MY FIRST BRITANNICA

Reference Guide and Index

13

ENCYCLOPÆDIA

Britannica®

CHICAGO   LONDON   NEW DELHI   PARIS   SEOUL   SYDNEY   TAIPEI   TOKYO

© 2004 by Encyclopædia Britannica, Inc.

International Standard Book Number: 1-59339-048-3 (set)
International Standard Book Number: 1-59339-061-0 (volume 13)

My First Britannica:
Volume 13: Reference Guide and Index 2004

Britannica.com may be accessed on the Internet at http://www.britannica.com.

Encyclopædia Britannica, and the Thistle logo are registered trademarks of Encyclopædia Britannica, Inc.

2437300

Reference Guide and Index

TABLE OF CONTENTS

At a glance...

My First Britannica is designed to be entertaining and informative. Presenting a broad spectrum of life on Earth and of the universe beyond, the set provides children with basic information about subjects they are interested in. The subjects have been specially chosen to convey a cross-cultural, international perspective. In addition, **My First Britannica** gives parents, teachers, and mentors an up-to-date reference with answers to the questions children are likely to ask.

My First Britannica consists of 12 main volumes, each organized around a broad subject area that in turn has connections to the subjects of other volumes:

© NASA

Science and Technology
The Earth and Earth Sciences, Volume 1
Physical Sciences and Technology, Volume 2

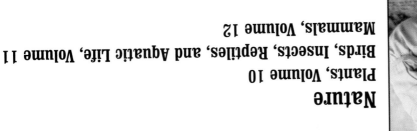
© Giacomo Pirozzi/Panos Pictures

People and Culture
The Arts, Volume 3
People in History, Volume 4
Folklore and Religions, Volume 5

© Christophe Loviny/Corbis

Places
Europe, Volume 6
Asia, Australia, and New Zealand, Volume 7
Africa, Volume 8
The Americas, Volume 9

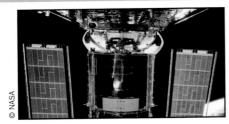
© Ariel Skelley/Corbis

Nature
Plants, Volume 10
Birds, Insects, Reptiles, and Aquatic Life, Volume 11
Mammals, Volume 12

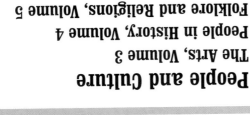

What this set covers

MY FIRST BRITANNICA is designed to hold children's attention with a highly visual presentation while building their study skills. The volumes may be read from cover to cover or used to find a specific fact. The Table of Contents at the beginning of each volume shows how the subject matter is organized and helps children browse through the volume or find information quickly.

Each volume of **My First BRITANNICA** is divided into two-page articles, or single spreads. The text of each article is written in an age-appropriate, engaging style that will capture the child's imagination while presenting him or her with just the right amount of information.

Included in each spread is a single vivid image or multiple images illustrating the subject and drawing the child in. These images consist of brilliant photographs, original illustrations, informative maps, and portraits of famous people.

Learn More! references at the end of each article point to related information in the same or other volumes. These references help children navigate through the set and understand the connections between subjects. For example, Australia is covered in Volume 7, but topics related to Australia can be found in other volumes as well:

■ Coral, Volume 11
■ Kangaroos, Volume 12
■ Kath Walker, Volume 3

Still others can be located by using the index to the set:

■ An Australian Tale: How Kangaroo Got His Tail, Volume 5
■ Eucalyptus, Volume 10
■ Koalas, Volume 12

Exploring interrelated topics from volume to volume will help children build their critical reasoning, comprehension, and vocabulary skills.

In this volume, the **Reference Guide and Index**, you will find a variety of useful reference tools, including a richly illustrated mini-atlas, a comprehensive glossary, and a cumulative index to the entire set. There is a helpful guide to using the index on pages 40-41, which shows children how the index is organized and how to find a specific subject. The index should be used along with the Table of Contents in each volume to locate a subject that is covered in more than one volume.

Although **My First BRITANNICA** covers a broad range of topics, it is not meant to be comprehensive. It is a fascinating resource, however, that children will want to read in its entirety and not just reach for when they want to look up a specific topic. As such, **My First BRITANNICA** will provide hours of pleasurable browsing for children and prepare them for more serious research in the future.

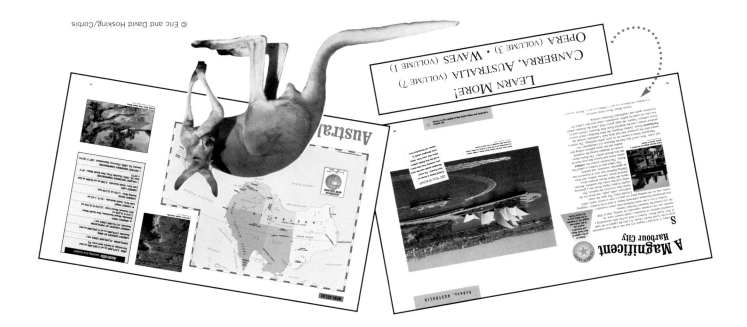

LEARN MORE!
CANBERRA, AUSTRALIA (VOLUME 7) • WAVES (VOLUME 1)
OPERA (VOLUME 3)

A Magnificent Harbour City

© Eric and David Hosking/Corbis

My First
BRITANNICA

Mini-
Atlas

AFRICA

Africa

AREA 30,347,000 sq km	
Percentage of Earth's land area: 20%	
POPULATION 826,835,999 (2002 est.)	
LARGEST COUNTRY BY AREA	
Sudan 2,504,000 sq km	
LARGEST COUNTRY BY POPULATION	
Nigeria 129,935,000	
▲ **HIGHEST POINT**	
Kilimanjaro, Tanzania 5,895 m	
▼ **LOWEST POINT**	
Lake Assal, Djibouti −157 m	
LONGEST RIVER	
Nile River 6,650 km	
LARGEST LAKE	
Lake Victoria 69,485 sq km	
X **COLDEST RECORDED TEMPERATURE**	
11 February 1935, Ifrane, Morocco −24°C	
X **HOTTEST RECORDED TEMPERATURE**	
13 September 1922, Al-Aziziyah, Libya 58°C	

Lake Assal, Djibouti.
© AFP/Corbis

The Cape of Good Hope is at the southern tip of Africa.
© Nik Wheeler/Corbis

Kilimanjaro, Tanzania.
© Yann Arthus-Bertrand/Corbis

The Nile River at the Aswan High Dam, Egypt.
© Lloyd Cluff/Corbis

Africa

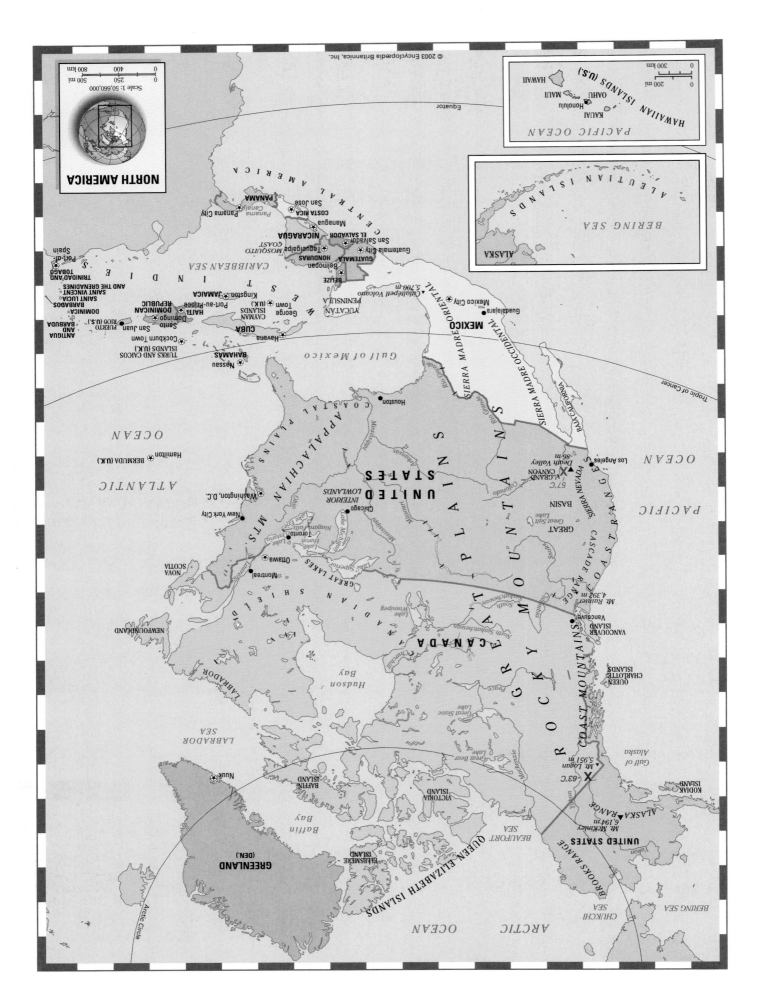

Death Valley, California, U.S.
© Royalty-Free/Corbis

Mount McKinley, Alaska, U.S.
© Jeff Vanuga/Corbis

North America

AREA 24,247,039 sq km
Percentage of Earth's land area: 16%

POPULATION 457,342,000 (2002 est.)

LARGEST COUNTRY BY AREA
Canada 9,984,700 sq km

LARGEST COUNTRY BY POPULATION
United States 287,602,000 (2002 est.)

▲ HIGHEST POINT
Mount McKinley, Alaska, U.S. 6,194 m

▼ LOWEST POINT
Death Valley, California, U.S. −86 m

LONGEST RIVER
Mississippi-Missouri River, U.S. 5,971 km

LARGEST LAKE
Lake Superior, U.S./Canada 82,100 sq km

X COLDEST RECORDED TEMPERATURE
3 February 1947, Snag, Yukon Territory, Canada −63°C

X HOTTEST RECORDED TEMPERATURE
10 July 1933, Death Valley, California, U.S. 57°C

Lowell Lake, Yukon Territory, Canada.
© Charlie Munsey/Corbis

Mississippi River at Iowa, U.S.
© David Muench/Corbis

North America

Amazon River, Brazil.
© Richard List/Corbis

An icy Mount Aconcagua, Argentina.
© S.P. Gillette/Corbis

South America

AREA 17,858,000 sq km
Percentage of Earth's land area: 12%

POPULATION 350,977,000 (2002 est.)

LARGEST COUNTRY BY AREA
Brazil 8,514,000 sq km

LARGEST COUNTRY BY POPULATION
Brazil 174,619,000 (2002 est.)

▲ HIGHEST POINT
Mount Aconcagua, Argentina 6,959 m

▼ LOWEST POINT
Valdez Peninsula, Argentina –40 m

LONGEST RIVER
Amazon River 6,400 km

LARGEST LAKE
Lake Maracaibo, Venezuela 13,280 sq km

X COLDEST RECORDED TEMPERATURE
1 June 1907, Sarmiento, Argentina –33°C

X HOTTEST RECORDED TEMPERATURE
11 December 1905, Rivadavia, Argentina 49°C

Lake Maracaibo, Venezuela.
© Yann Arthus-Bertrand/Corbis

South America

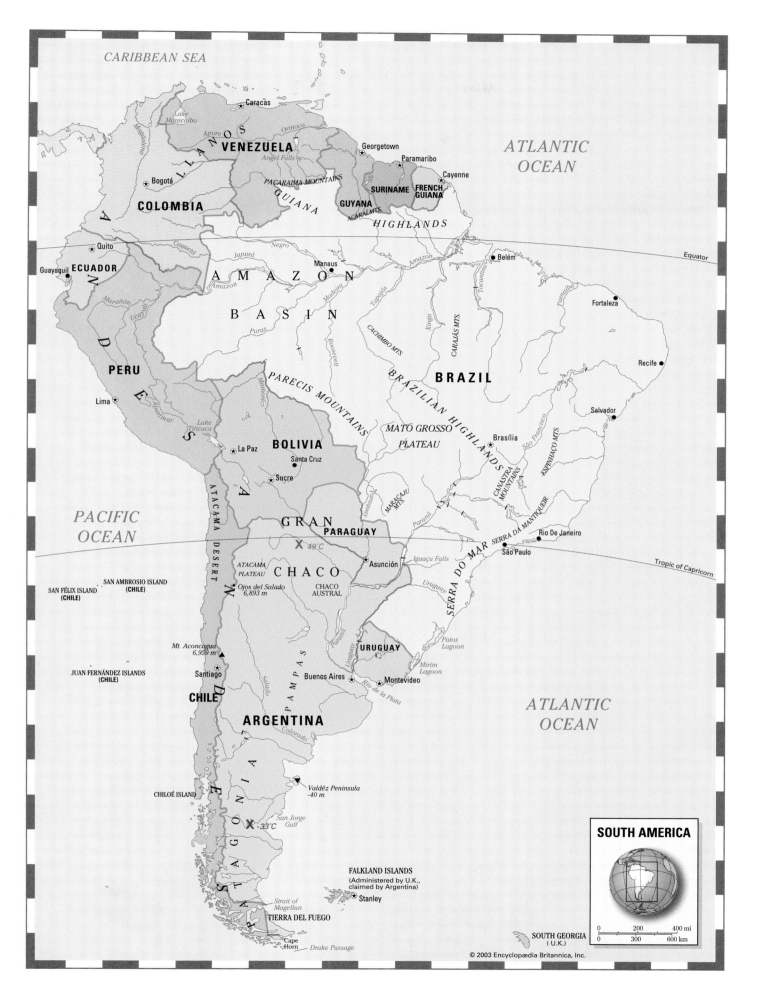

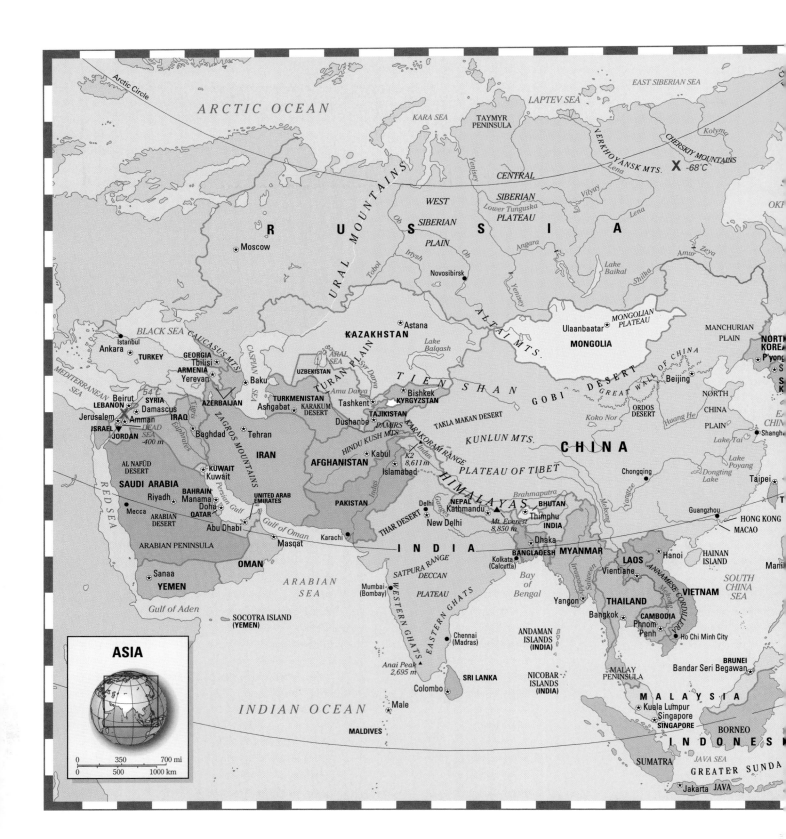

Asia

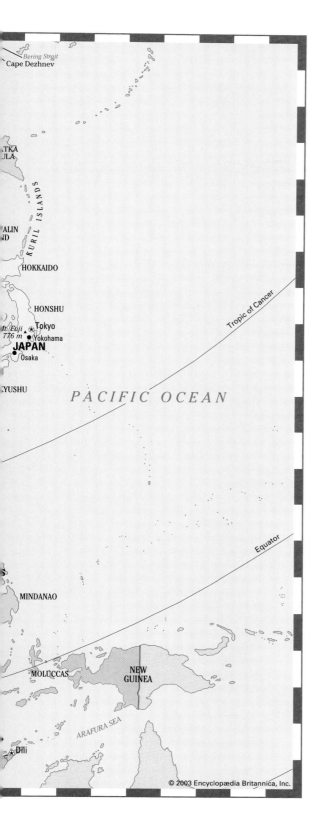

Bering Strgit
Cape Dezhnev

'TKA
'JLA

'ALIN
'ID

KURIL ISLANDS

HOKKAIDO

HONSHU

Mt. Fuji
776 m
Tokyo
Yokohama
JAPAN
Osaka

KYUSHU

PACIFIC OCEAN

Tropic of Cancer

Equator

MINDANAO

MOLUCCAS
NEW
GUINEA

ARAFURA SEA

Dili

© 2003 Encyclopædia Britannica, Inc.

Asia

AREA 44,614,000 sq km
Percentage of Earth's land area: 30%

POPULATION 3,772,000,000 (2001 est.)

LARGEST COUNTRY BY AREA
Russia (Siberia) 13,119,600 sq km

LARGEST COUNTRY BY POPULATION
China 1,284,211,000 (2002 est.)

▲ HIGHEST POINT
Mount Everest 8,850 m

▼ LOWEST POINT
Dead Sea −400 m

LONGEST RIVER
Yangtze River, China 6,300 km

LARGEST LAKE
Caspian Sea (Asia/Europe) 371,000 sq km

X COLDEST RECORDED TEMPERATURE
6 February 1933, Oymyakon, Russia −68°C

X HOTTEST RECORDED TEMPERATURE
21 June 1942, Tirat Zevi, Israel 54°C

Mount Everest, Nepal and China.
© David Keaton/Corbis

Yangtze River flowing on the Plateau of Tibet, China.
© How-Man Wong/Corbis

13

Europe

AREA 10,400,000 sq km
Percentage of Earth's land area: 7%

POPULATION 666,498,000 (2001 est.)

LARGEST COUNTRY BY AREA
Russia (European) 3,955,900 sq km

LARGEST COUNTRY BY POPULATION
Russia (European) 104,472,000 (2001 est.)

HIGHEST POINT
Mount Elbrus, Russia 5,642 m [off map]

LOWEST POINT
Caspian Sea −28.5 m [off map]

LONGEST RIVER
Volga River, Russia 3,530 km

LARGEST LAKE
Caspian Sea (Europe/Asia)
371,000 sq km [off map]

COLDEST RECORDED TEMPERATURE
January (exact date unknown),
Ust-Shchugor, Russia −55°C [off map]

X HOTTEST RECORDED TEMPERATURE
4 August 1881, Sevilla, Spain 49°C

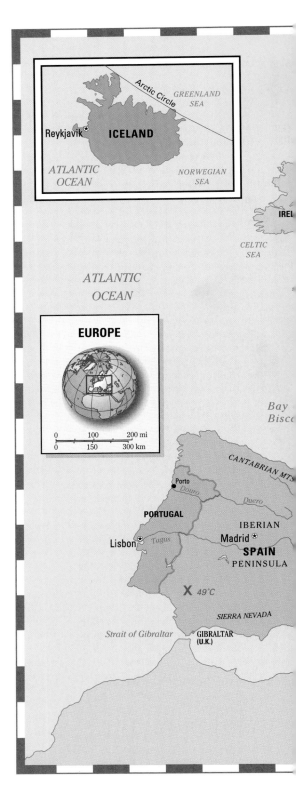

**Mont Blanc, France,
Europe's second
highest point.**
© Ludovic Maisant/Corbis

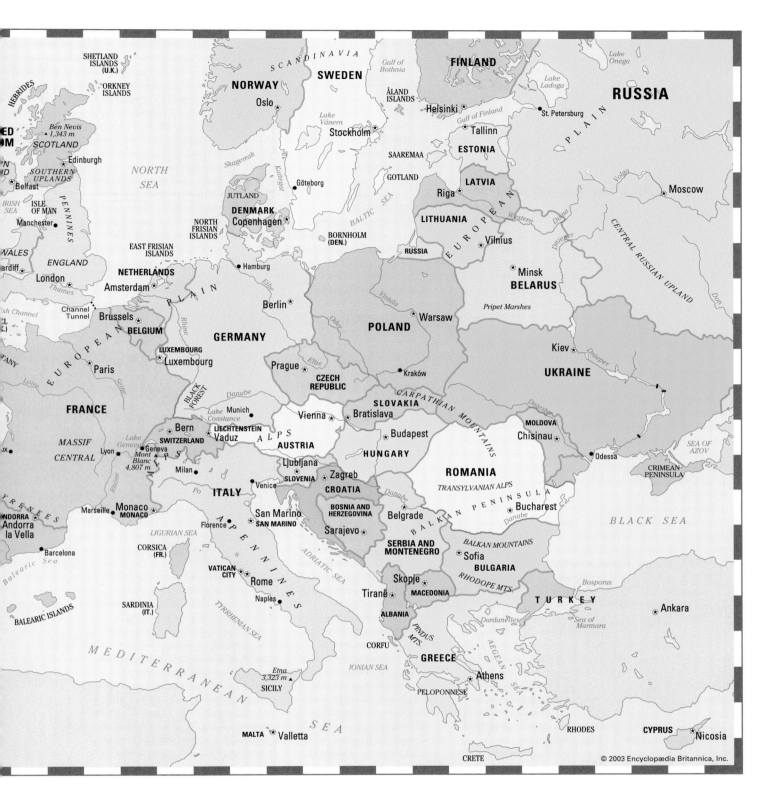

SHETLAND ISLANDS (U.K.)

HEBRIDES

ORKNEY ISLANDS

ED OM

SCOTLAND

Ben Nevis ▲ 1,343 m

Edinburgh

SOUTHERN UPLANDS

ND

Belfast

IRISH SEA

ISLE OF MAN

PENNINES

Manchester

WALES

ardiff

ENGLAND

London

Thames

Channel Tunnel

EL .)

English Channel

ANY

NORTH SEA

SCANDINAVIA

NORWAY

Oslo

Skagerrak

Kattegat

JUTLAND

Göteborg

DENMARK

Copenhagen

NORTH FRISIAN ISLANDS

EAST FRISIAN ISLANDS

NETHERLANDS

Amsterdam

Hamburg

Elbe

Brussels

BELGIUM

EUROPEAN

PLAIN

LUXEMBOURG

Luxembourg

Paris

Loire

Saône

GERMANY

Berlin

Oder

Rhine

BLACK FOREST

Danube

Prague

Elbe

CZECH REPUBLIC

FRANCE

Munich

Lake Constance

MASSIF CENTRAL

Lyon

Bern

SWITZERLAND

LIECHTENSTEIN

Vaduz

Lake Geneva

Geneva

Mont Blanc 4,807 m

Milan

ALPS

Rhône

Po

ITALY

Venice

SLOVENIA

Ljubljana

Zagreb

CROATIA

SWEDEN

Lake Vänern

Stockholm

BALTIC SEA

BORNHOLM (DEN.)

Vistula

POLAND

Warsaw

Kraków

SLOVAKIA

Vienna

Bratislava

AUSTRIA

Budapest

HUNGARY

Danube

CARPATHIAN MOUNTAINS

Gulf of Bothnia

ÅLAND ISLANDS

SAAREMAA

GOTLAND

Riga

LITHUANIA

RUSSIA

Vilnius

Western

FINLAND

Helsinki

Tallinn

ESTONIA

LATVIA

Dvina

Lake Onega

Lake Ladoga

St. Petersburg

RUSSIA

EUROPEAN

Dnieper

Minsk

BELARUS

Pripet Marshes

Kiev

UKRAINE

Dniester

Chisinau

MOLDOVA

Odessa

PLAIN

Volga

Moscow

CENTRAL RUSSIAN UPLAND

Don

Dnieper

SEA OF AZOV

CRIMEAN PENINSULA

PYRENEES

IX

ANDORRA

Andorra la Vella

Marseille

Monaco

MONACO

LIGURIAN SEA

Florence

APENNINES

CORSICA (FR.)

Barcelona

Balearic SEA

San Marino

SAN MARINO

VATICAN CITY

Rome

SARDINIA (IT.)

BALEARIC ISLANDS

San Marino

TYRRHENIAN SEA

Naples

Belgrade

BOSNIA AND HERZEGOVINA

Sarajevo

SERBIA AND MONTENEGRO

Danube

ROMANIA

TRANSYLVANIAN ALPS

Bucharest

BALKAN PENINSULA

Danube

BALKAN MOUNTAINS

Sofia

BULGARIA

Skopje

MACEDONIA

ALBANIA

Tiranë

RHODOPE MTS.

BLACK SEA

Bosporus

TURKEY

Ankara

Dardanelles

Sea of Marmara

AEGEAN SEA

MEDITERRANEAN

Etna 3,323 m ▲

SICILY

PINDUS MTS.

CORFU

GREECE

Athens

IONIAN SEA

PELOPONNESE

SEA

MALTA

Valletta

RHODES

CRETE

CYPRUS

Nicosia

© 2003 Encyclopædia Britannica, Inc.

Volga River, Russia.
© Buddy Mays/Corbis

Sevilla, Spain.
© Nik Wheeler/Corbis

Europe

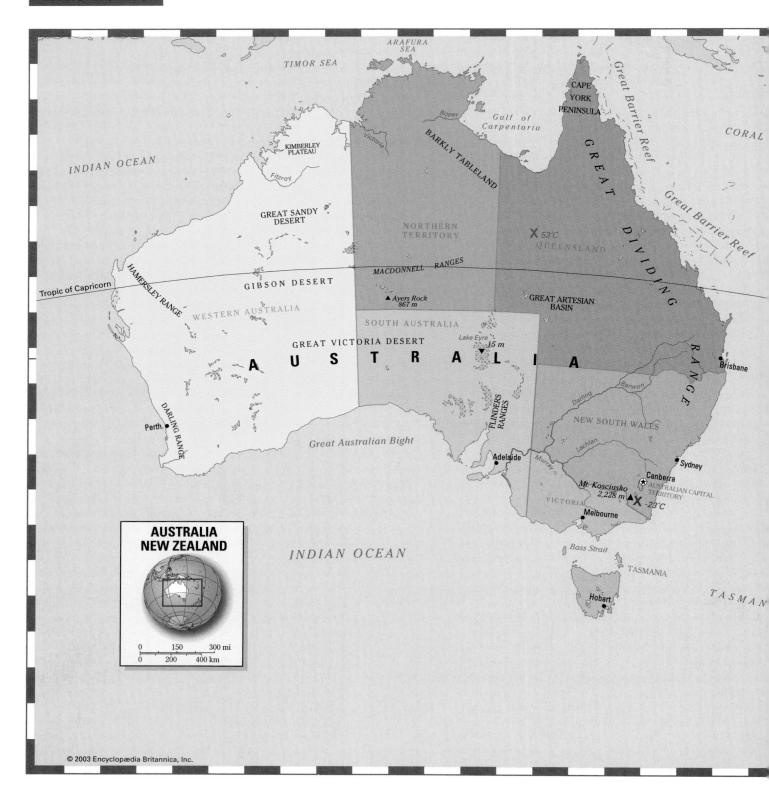

TIMOR SEA

ARAFURA
SEA

INDIAN OCEAN

CAPE
YORK
PENINSULA

Great Barrier Reef

CORAL

Roper

Gulf of
Carpentaria

KIMBERLEY
PLATEAU

Fitzroy

Victoria

BARKLY TABLELAND

Great Barrier Reef

GREAT SANDY
DESERT

NORTHERN
TERRITORY

G
R
E
A
T

X 53°C
QUEENSLAND

D
I
V
I
D
I
N
G

MACDONNELL RANGES

Tropic of Capricorn

HAMERSLEY RANGE

GIBSON DESERT

▲ Ayers Rock
867 m

GREAT ARTESIAN
BASIN

R
A
N
G
E

WESTERN AUSTRALIA

SOUTH AUSTRALIA

GREAT VICTORIA DESERT

Lake Eyre
-15 m

A U S T R A L I A

Brisbane

DARLING RANGE

Perth.

Great Australian Bight

FLINDERS
RANGES

Darling

Barwon

NEW SOUTH WALES

Lachlan

Sydney

Adelaide

Murray

Canberra
AUSTRALIAN CAPITAL
TERRITORY

Mt. Kosciusko
2,228 m ▲X
-23°C

INDIAN OCEAN

VICTORIA

Melbourne

Bass Strait

TASMANIA

TASMAN

Hobart

**AUSTRALIA
NEW ZEALAND**

| 0 | 150 | 300 mi |
| 0 | 200 | 400 km |

Australia

Lake Eyre, South Australia.
© Ted Spiegel/Corbis

Australia (including New Zealand)

AREA 7,962,000 sq km
Percentage of Earth's land area: 5%

POPULATION 23,595,000 (2002 est.)

LARGEST COUNTRY BY AREA
Australia 7,692,000 sq km

LARGEST COUNTRY BY POPULATION
Australia 19,702,000 (2002 est.)

▲ HIGHEST POINT
Australia: Mount Kosciusko, New South Wales 2,228 m
New Zealand: Mount Cook 3,754 m

▼ LOWEST POINT
Lake Eyre, South Australia −15 m

LONGEST RIVER
Darling River 2,739 km

LARGEST LAKE
Lake Eyre, South Australia 9,600 sq km

X COLDEST RECORDED TEMPERATURE
29 June 1994, Charlotte Pass, New South Wales −23°C

X HOTTEST RECORDED TEMPERATURE
16 January 1889, Cloncurry, Queensland 53°C

ACIFIC OCEAN

Auckland

North Island

NEW ZEALAND

▲ Mt. Ruapehu
2,797 m

⊛ Wellington

Mt. Cook
3,754 m ▲

Cook Strait

Southern Alps

● Christchurch

South Island

Darling River, New South Wales.
© Michael & Patricia Fogden/Corbis

Snowy peaks on the Antarctic coast.
© George D. Lepp/Corbis

Antarctica

Antarctica	
AREA 14,245,000 sq km **Percentage of Earth's land area: 9%**	
POPULATION No permanent population	
▲ HIGHEST POINT Vinson Massif 4,897 m	
▼ LOWEST POINT Bentley Subglacial Trench −2,538 m	
X COLDEST RECORDED TEMPERATURE 21 July 1983, Vostock Station −89°C	
X HOTTEST RECORDED TEMPERATURE 5 January 1974, Lake Vanda 15°C	

Water-filled crater in Antarctica.
© Peter Johnson/Corbis

Crater of Mount Erebus, Ross Island, Antarctica.
© Galen Rowell/Corbis

Biologist walks through mountains of Cape Crozier, Antarctica.
© Galen Rowell/Corbis

Antarctica

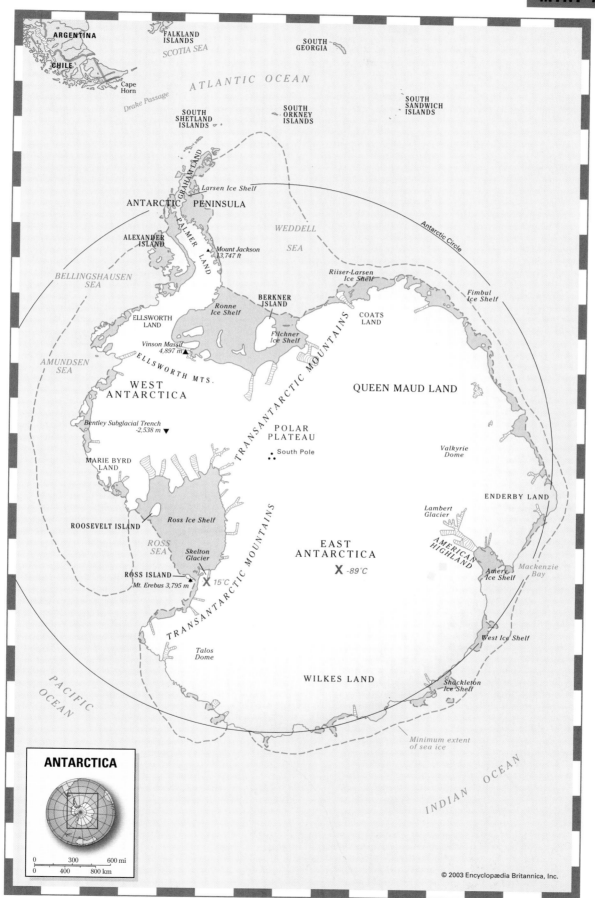

MINI-ATLAS

ANTARCTICA

© 2003 Encyclopædia Britannica, Inc.

19

G L O S S A R Y

abandon to leave without planning to return

abbey place where a community of monks or nuns live and work; also, the church serving that community

abdomen in insects, the end portion of the body that is behind the head and thorax (middle section)

abominable horrible or disgusting

Aboriginal having to do with the original people to live in an area; especially, the original peoples of Australia

absorb soak up

abstract (adjective) in the arts, creatively communicating feelings or ideas about a subject rather than creating a realistic image

abundance great quantity; plenty

abyssal having to do with an area of the ocean that is thousands of metres below the surface of the water

acid a chemical substance, often producing a burning effect when it interacts with another material

acrobat performer who does tricks and physical routines that require strength, balance, and body control, often above the ground

acrylic type of paint

adaptation change in an organism or its parts that allows the organism to survive better in its environment

administrative having to do with managing or supervising the functions of a business, organization, or government

aerial metallic rod or wire for sending or receiving radio waves or other energy signals

aerial acrobat performer who does tricks and feats above the ground or in the air, especially on a trapeze

affordable reasonable in price

agent something that produces an effect

aggressive openly hostile or tending to approach with great force or energy

agriculture farming

alas unfortunately or sadly

algae (singular: **alga**) group of organisms that are similar to plants and live mostly in the water

alpine mountainous

altar raised place on which sacrifices are offered or religious ceremonies are performed

altitude the distance of an object above a specific level (such as sea level) on a planet or other heavenly body

ambassador person who officially represents his or her own government in a foreign country

amphitheatre building with seats rising in curved rows around an open space where games and plays take place

ancestry all the family members who lived before a particular individual

antenna (plural: **antennae**) in biology, a slender organ on the head of some insects and crustaceans (such as shrimps and lobsters) that allows them to sense their environment

anticlockwise in the direction opposite to the way a clock's hands move, as viewed from the front

antics playful or funny actions

Arab member of a people originating in the Arabian Peninsula and now inhabiting much of the Middle East and North Africa

arc a curved line

archaeology (adjective: **archaeological**) the science that deals with past human life as shown by fossils, tools, and other material left by ancient peoples

archbishop high-ranking churchman in some Christian churches who supervises church government in a very large area

architecture the art of designing and building structures, especially buildings that can be lived and worked in

archives place where public records or historical documents are kept

arena enclosed area used for public entertainment

aristocratic having to do with the upper social classes

artificial made by human beings rather than occurring in nature

aspect part, feature, or quality of something

asteroid small, often rock-like heavenly body orbiting the Sun

astronomy (adjective: **astronomical**) the science of the heavenly bodies and of their sizes, motions, and composition

atmosphere the envelope of gases that surrounds a planet

autobiography life story written by the person it is about

autonomous independent and self-governing

axis imaginary pole going through the centre of the Earth or other heavenly body

bacterium (plural: **bacteria**) tiny one-celled organism too small to see with the unaided eye

baleen a hardened substance from 0.6 to 3.6 metres long found in two rows along the upper jaws of certain whales

banish to force or drive away

barrier object or structure that blocks the ability to reach another object or place

basilica Roman Catholic church that has special ceremonial privileges

basin in geography, the area of land drained by a river and its branches

bask to lie or relax in a warm place

bay part of a coastline that curves in towards land

bazaar marketplace where many kinds of goods are sold; *especially*, such a marketplace in Asia or Africa

Berber member or descendant of a people who originally inhabited North Africa, before the Arab conquest in the 7th century AD

betray to lie to or go back on one's word

biologist person who studies living organisms and life processes

blockbuster huge, successful event

bog wet spongy ground

bond connection or friendship

botanical (noun: **botany**) having to do with plant life

boulevard wide avenue often having grass strips with trees along its centre or sides

bovine animal group that includes cattle, oxen, bison, and buffalo

boycott the refusal to deal with a person, group, or country, usually in order to show disapproval or to force a change in behaviour

Braille a system of writing for the blind in which letters are represented by raised dots

bray to make a sound like the loud harsh call of a donkey

breadth width

brew to prepare by steeping (soaking) or boiling in hot water

broadcast to send out a programme or message to a group, usually by radio, television, or the Internet

buff an off-white colour

burden weight or load to carry

burrow deep hole or tunnel made in the ground by an animal for shelter

bushman in Australia, a person who lives in the bush (wilderness)

cactus flowering plant of dry regions that has water-storing fleshy stems and, usually, sharp spines

calorie unit that measures the amount of heat energy that food provides to the body

camouflage colours and patterns that allow a person, animal, or thing to blend in with the surroundings

campaign planned activities designed to lead to a particular result

canal artificial waterway for boats or for draining or supplying water to land

canoe a small, light, and narrow boat having sharp front and back ends and moved by paddling

canopy overhead covering

captive (noun: **captivity**) (adjective) taken and held in a cage or as a prisoner; (noun) one who has been taken or held in a cage or as a prisoner

caravan group of pack animals or of vehicles travelling together one behind the other

carbohydrates plentiful, energy-producing natural substances that are formed by many food plants eaten by animals

carcass dead body or leftover parts of an animal

cargo goods transported in a ship, airplane, or other vehicle

cartridge sealed container

cassava tropical plant that has a thick underground root-like part and can be made into a number of foods

cast (verb) to form a shape by pouring a liquid into a mould and letting it harden

cathedral large Christian church where a bishop is in charge

ceramics objects made out of clay baked at high temperatures

cereal starchy seeds of certain grass plants grown for food

chairman person who leads a meeting or an organization

champagne a sparkling white wine

channel narrow passageway between two areas of water

chapel small, sometimes private place for prayer or special religious services

charitable done to serve the needs of the poor or sick

château castle or large country house, especially in France

chemical one of the combined substances making up living and nonliving things

chemist scientist who studies the make-up and properties of physical substances and the changes that they go through

choreographer creator of a dance

circulate to flow

citadel castle or fortress that protects a city

citrus kind of tree or shrub grown in warm regions and having thick rind (skin) and fleshy fruits, including oranges, grapefruits, and lemons

civil rights the social and personal rights of a citizen

civil war war between opposing groups of citizens of the same country

civilization the way of life of a people at a particular time or place; also, a fairly advanced culture and technology

classical traditional in style

climate average weather in a particular area

clockwise in the direction that a clock's hands move, as viewed from the front

cloudburst sudden heavy rainfall

cobbled made of rounded stones larger than a pebble and smaller than a boulder

colony (adjective: **colonial**; verb: **colonize**) 1) in general, a settlement established in a distant territory and controlled by a more powerful and expanding nation; 2) in biology, a group of similar organisms that live together in a particular place

comet chunk of frozen space debris that has a shiny tail and orbits the Sun

commanding grand and powerful

commandment law or rule for living

commerce (adjective: **commercial**) the buying and selling of goods, especially on a large scale and between different places

commission (verb) to order to be made; (noun) an order granting the power to perform various acts or duties

commoner person who is not of the noble or upper classes

communism (adjective: **communist**) system of government in which all property is owned by the state or community and all citizens are supposed to have a share in the total wealth

composer person who writes music

composition literary, musical, or other artistic work

concentrated condensed, or made thicker, by removing water

conductor the leader of an orchestra

conflict disagreement, struggle, or fighting

congress the main law-making group of some nations

conquistador (plural: **conquistadores**) a Spanish conqueror of Latin America

conservation the care and protection of something fragile, unique, and valuable, such as rare wildlife or ancient structures

conservative tending to safeguard existing views, conditions, or traditions

constitution document containing the basic beliefs and laws of a nation, state, or social group

continent one of the largest of Earth's landmasses

contour the outline of a figure, body, or surface

contract (verb) to make smaller by tightening or squeezing together

controversial causing division or disagreement

convert to change; to win over to a new or different belief

conveyor belt a loop of material that can move objects from one worker or workstation to the next for the steps needed to make a product

convict (noun) person serving a prison sentence

core central part

corkscrew device with a handle and a spiral-twist metal piece, used for removing certain bottle stoppers

corridor passageway into which compartments or rooms open

countless too many to count

craft (noun) a skill or trade; (verb) to make skillfully, usually by hand

crater bowl-shaped dent in a surface

crest (adjective: **crested**) 1) in biology, a standing clump of fur or feathers, usually on an animal's head; 2) in geography, the upper edge or limit of something, such as the top of a mountain

critic person who studies and comments on the quality of performances or works of art

crossbreed to produce offspring from parents of two varieties or species

crossroads place where roads cross; also, a central meeting place or a decision-making point

crown prince (feminine: **crown princess**) the prince next in line for a crown or throne

crude oil oil taken from the ground and not yet cleaned or separated into different products; also called petroleum

cruise a pleasure trip on a large boat or ship

crusade campaign or cause taken up with passion and belief

crystal clear colourless glass of very good quality

cuisine style of cooking; also, foods made in that style

cultivate in gardening and farming, to plant crops and to care for them as they grow

culture the ways of life, traditions, and behaviours of a specific group of people

customhouse place where duties or taxes are paid on goods coming into or leaving a country

cutting in gardening and farming, a section of an adult plant capable of developing into a new individual

Cyrillic having to do with the alphabet for writing in Russian and other Eastern European languages

data factual information or details

dean in education, the head of a division of a school or university

debris rubbish or fragments

debut first formal public appearance

decade ten-year period

delta large triangular area made of material deposited at the mouth of a river, where it empties into the sea

democracy (adjective: **democratic**) government in which the highest power is held by the citizens; they either use their power directly (usually by voting) or choose others to act for them

depict to represent by a picture

deposit substance laid down by a natural process

deputy member of a law-making group in some nations

descendant member of a recent age group of a family or similar division that began years earlier

descended (adjective) related through a long line of ancestors

descent ancestry, heritage, or origin

devastate to wreck or destroy

device tool or piece of equipment

devise to work out, invent, or plan

dialect one of several varieties of a language used by the members of a particular group or class of people

dialogue conversation in a play, film, or written work

diameter the length of a straight line through the centre of an object

dictate to speak for another person to write down or for a machine to record

dictator person who rules with total power, often in a cruel or brutal way

diesel type of fuel-fed engine

digestive system parts of the body that work together to break down food into simpler forms that can be used by the body

diplomat person who works to keep up friendly relations between the governments of different countries

disc in plants, the central part of certain flower heads, as in daisies and sunflowers; the discs, in turn, are surrounded by ray flowers

discrimination treating some individuals or groups differently from others without any fair or proper reason

dismay sadness or disappointment

dispute (verb) to argue with

diverse varied; different

divine holy, godlike, or concerning God

dome large rounded structure shaped like half of a ball

domestic (verb: **domesticate**) tame

dominant having influence or control over another person, place, or thing

drastic huge, extreme, or dramatic

drawback problem or bad side

drought long period of dry weather

dual two

duct pipe, tube, or channel through which liquid or gases flow

dung animal waste

dwindle to become smaller or less

dyke mound of earth built to control water

dynasty series of rulers of the same family

echo (verb) to repeat or imitate a sound

economical inexpensive and efficient

economy the system in a country or group by which goods are made, services are offered, and both are sold and used

ecosystem community of all the living things in a region, their physical environment, and all their interrelationships

edict law or order given by a ruler or leader

edit to cut down to a different or shorter version

effortless easy and natural

element in science, one of the basic unique substances that make up all matter

elevation the height of an object above sea level (that is, the surface of the ocean)

embassy the living quarters or office of an ambassador (a person who officially represents his or her own government in a foreign country)

embroidery needlework done to decorate cloth

emperor (feminine: **empress**) the ruler of an empire

empire a major widespread area under a single government, or a number of territories or peoples under one supreme ruler

endangered species a group of plants or animals whose entire survival is threatened

energetic lively or active

engineer person who is trained to design and produce complex structures such as roads, bridges, and dams

enlightenment remarkably clear state of awareness, understanding, and inner peace

equator imaginary circle running east-to-west around the Earth that lies halfway between the North Pole and the South Pole

erosion (verb: **erode**) the process of wearing down; *especially*, the wearing away of soil or rock by wind, water, or ice

ethnic having to do with a large group of people who share a racial, national, tribal, religious, language, or cultural background

ethnography (adjective: **ethnographic**) the study of human cultures

evaporate change into a vapour or gaseous form, usually by means of heating

evergreen (adjective) having leaves that remain green and working through winter and more than one growing season

evolution (verb: **evolve**) the process of changing, especially over time

exile (noun) banishment or official separation

exotic unusual and unfamiliar

expanse large area

expedition a planned journey or trip made for a specific purpose

export to carry or send abroad, especially for sale in another country

expression communication, usually of emotions or ideas

extend to stretch out or reach across a distance, space, or time

extinct no longer existing

extremist person who holds unusually strong opinions or beliefs

famine drastic food shortage, often ending in starvation for many

fantastical highly imaginative and unrealistic

fast (noun) period of time when a person gives up or limits eating, often for religious reasons

ferocious fierce and wild

fertile rich and productive; able to yield quality crops in large quantities

fertilizer natural or artificial substance used to make soil better for growing crops

fibre strand or thread-like structure

fix in photography, to make an image lasting

flare (verb) to fan out or expand

flask container for liquid

flax the fibre from which linen cloth is made

fleece wool of an animal such as a sheep or a goat

flourish to grow successfully; to do well

fodder coarse food for farm animals

foliage the leaves of a plant

forefoot one of the front feet of an animal with four or more feet

forestry the science and work of caring for forests

formal following a specific order or pattern

fortify to strengthen with weapons and by military defences

fortress well-defended place

fossil an imprint or other trace in rock of an animal, plant, or other living thing

foundation the support on which something rests; also, the base from which an idea or creation grows

fragrance (adjective: **fragrant**) sweet, pleasant, and often flowery or fruity smell

frankincense a sweet-smelling substance from an African or Arabian tree

fresco painting done on freshly spread moist plaster

frigid frozen or extremely cold

fungus (plural: **fungi**) organism (such as a mushroom or mould) similar to a plant but lacking a stem, roots, leaves, and the substance called 'chlorophyll'

fuse an electrical safety device

fusion the blending or combination of two or more things, as if melted together

gallery room or building that is used to display special objects or works of art

gangster member of a gang of criminals

gear a toothed wheel that works as part of a machine

gemstone natural material that can be cut and polished for use in jewellery

generate to create or be the cause of

geography the natural physical features of an area; also, the study of the countries of the world and of the Earth's surface features

geometric based on straight lines, curves, and simple shapes such as circles and squares

gesture movement of the body, arms, hands, or legs to express feelings or thoughts

gills pair of breathing organs found in fish and some other water-dwelling animals

glacier large river-like body of ice moving slowly down a slope or spreading over a land surface

gladiator in ancient Rome, a person who fought to the death as part of a public entertainment

gland structure in animals that produces special substances, such as sweat or oil or milk

glider soaring aircraft similar to an airplane but without an engine

global warming increase in the average temperature on the planet Earth

gorge narrow steep-walled canyon

gory violent and bloody

Gospel one of the first four New Testament books of the Bible, telling of the life, death, and resurrection (raising from the dead) of Jesus Christ

gospel, or **gospel music** black American music that grew mostly from Christian church services, blues, and traditional spirituals

governess woman who teaches and trains a child in a private home

gravity force that attracts objects to each other, keeps people and objects anchored to the ground, and keeps planets circling the Sun

guerrilla person who is part of an independent fighting force that makes surprise raids behind enemy lines

gymnastics difficult physical exercises, often performed as a sport in competitions

habitat the physical environment in which a living thing dwells

hail small balls or lumps of ice that fall from the sky, as rain does

handicrafts articles, such as pottery, made by hand by an individual person

handiwork creative product

hare rabbit-like animal

harness (verb) to control, much as an animal may be hitched up and controlled by its harness

harvest the gathering of a crop

hatch to come forth from an egg or other protective covering during development

headquarters the governing and directing centre of an organization

heath low evergreen shrub with needle-like leaves and clusters of small flowers

hemisphere half of the planet Earth or any other globe-shaped object

herb pleasant-smelling plant (such as mint, oregano, basil, and coriander) often used in cooking, either in part or as a whole

heritage background or descent

hermit person who has withdrawn from society to live alone

hibernate to pass the winter in a sleeping or resting state

highland high or mountainous land

horizon distant point where the land and the sky appear to meet

hot spring a source of hot water coming from underground

hull hard outer shell of a seed; also, the outer layer of a boat or ship

humanitarian devoted to the happiness and welfare of other people

humidity (adjective: **humid**) moisture or dampness; *especially*, the amount of moisture in the air

hurricane major tropical storm that occurs in the Atlantic Ocean and features high winds moving in circular patterns; in the Pacific Ocean such storms are called 'typhoons'

husk usually thin, dry outer covering of a fruit or seed

hymn song of joy or praise, often to a god

immigrant person who goes to a country to live there

immigration the process of moving to a new country

immortal living or lasting forever

impaired damaged or limited

imperial having to do with an empire or emperor

impish playfully naughty

implant (noun) object inserted within living tissue; (verb) to insert securely or deeply

import to bring from a foreign place

impression mark or figure made by pressing one object onto the surface of another; also, the effect or feeling an object or person creates

inanimate not living

incense substance that produces a sweet smell when burned

indivisible unable to be divided

industrial having to do with businesses that construct or produce something

Industrial Revolution 18th-century era that began when power-driven machinery became common

industrialized built up and modernized through business and manufacturing

industry business and manufacturing

inhabited (adjective) occupied; having residents

inhaler device through which medicine is drawn in through the nose or mouth

inlaid decorated with materials set into the surface

inland part of a country away from the coast

inspiration something that causes a particular thought, feeling, or idea

instinct natural tendency of a living thing to respond in a particular way to a situation

integrate (adjective: **integrated**) to combine two or more parts in order to create a more balanced whole; *especially*, to remove barriers that isolate one group of people from another

international having to do with two or more countries

intricate complicated or detailed

investigate to look into or study

islet small island

isolate to keep separate or alone

isthmus narrow strip of land connecting two larger land areas

ivory material that makes up elephant and walrus tusks

judo sport, developed from the Japanese fighting art of *jujitsu*, in which opponents use quick movements and careful positioning to try to throw each other to the ground

kernel whole grain or seed of a cereal plant

laboratory place where science tests and experiments are done

landmass large area of land

landscape picture showing views of nature and the countryside

larva (plural: **larvae**) wingless, often wormlike stage of many insects

lash to tie or attach

layperson (adjective: **lay**) person who belongs to a religious group but is not part of its official clergy (as a priest or minister is)

legacy something handed down from an earlier time or person

legislature an organized government group with the power to make laws

lens (plural: **lenses**) curved piece of glass that concentrates rays of light

liberation freedom

literacy the ability to read and write

litter group of newborn animals born to the same mother at the same time

livestock animals kept or reared, especially farm animals such as cattle, pigs, sheep, goats, and horses

locomotive railway vehicle that carries the engine that moves train cars along

loot to steal from a home or public place, especially during rioting or wartime

lunar having to do with the Moon

lung organ that helps some animals breathe air

lyrics the words of a song

magistrate official who looks after the laws of a particular area

magnify to make something appear larger

majestic grand or splendid

majority most; usually, more than half of a group of individual people or things

majority rule system in which the majority (that is, a number over half) of a group is given the power to make decisions that the entire group must accept

mammal class of warm-blooded animals that feed their young with milk from special mammary glands, have an internal backbone, and are more or less covered with hair

mangrove tropical tree or shrub that has partly exposed roots and grows thickly in areas of salty water

manufacture to make from raw materials, by hand or by machine

manuscript handwritten or typewritten document

marginal lying at or near the outer edge (margin) of some larger place, object, or group

marine having to do with the ocean

marmalade clear, usually sugary jelly containing pieces of fruit and fruit rind

marsh area of soft wet land usually overgrown by grasses and sedges

massive heavy or large

matter physical substance or material from which something is made

mausoleum large or fancy tomb

meal coarsely ground substance

medicinal used as a medicine

medieval period in European history from the 5th to about the 14th century AD

meditation (verb: **meditate**) quiet, focussed concentration, meant to calm and clear the mind; sometimes used to reach a spiritual awareness

memorial something that keeps alive the memory of a person or event

mesa flat-topped hill or small upland with steep sides

meteorite mass of material from space that reaches the Earth's surface

method way or system

metropolitan having to do with a city and its heavily populated surrounding areas

microphone device that changes sound to electrical signals, usually in order to record or send sound

migration movement from one country or place to another

minaret in Islamic architecture, the tall slender tower of a mosque, from which Muslims are called to prayer

mineral substance that is not animal or plant and is an important nutrient for living things

mischievous playfully naughty

moccasin soft leather shoe first worn by Native American Indians

module independent unit made to be part of a larger structure

molecules the smallest possible pieces of a particular substance

mollusc any member of a group of animals that have no backbone and are usually enclosed in a shell (for example, snails, clams, or squids)

molten melted

monarchy form of government in which the ruler inherits the position and rules for life; monarchs include kings, queens, emperors, and tsars

monastery housing for people who have taken religious vows, especially for monks

monk man who lives separately from society, either alone or in a community of men, so that he can devote all his time to religious life

monsoon regular period of heavy rainfall and wind, especially in southern Asia

monument stone or building set up in memory of a person or event

mosque Muslim place of worship

mountaineer mountain climber

mourn to feel great sorrow, usually because of a death or other loss

mural a painting on a wall

mussel kind of mollusc (shellfish)

muzzle animal's snout (jaw and nose)

mystical having to do with a person's direct spiritual connection with a god or other supernatural power

myth story that unfolds part of the worldview of a people or is used to explain a belief or natural event

mythology the stories dealing with the gods and heroes of a particular people or culture

native (adjective) living or growing naturally in a particular region

natural resources the materials or qualities supplied by nature (such as minerals or water power) that make a place valuable to people, usually for industrial and manufacturing purposes

nature inborn or instinctive way of behaving or thinking

nectar sweet liquid produced by plants and used by bees in making honey

negotiate to discuss and bargain with another in order to reach an agreement

Negro spiritual religious folk song developed among blacks in the southern United States

network complex system

nobility a nation's upper-class social group

noble of upper-class birth or rank

nocturnal active at night

nomad member of a people who have no permanent home but instead move from place to place, usually with the seasons and within a specific area

non-fiction literature that is based on fact rather than imagination

nostril one of the outer openings of the nose

nuclear weapon explosive device that produces enormous power by splitting apart the centres of the tiny particles called 'atoms'

nuisance annoying or troublesome person, thing, or event

nursery place where plants are grown for farming, for scientific experiments, or for sale to the public

nutrient substance that a living thing needs in order to stay healthy and grow

ocelot medium-sized wildcat of the Americas

oddity unusual thing or quality

oral having to do with the mouth

orbit (verb) to travel around an object; (noun) an object's path around another object

orchestra group of musicians playing together, usually with a leader called a 'conductor'

order religious community, usually requiring that its members take solemn vows promising duty and faithfulness

organism living thing

organization group of people working together for some purpose

orthodox strictly obeying traditional rules, customs, or beliefs

overseer person in charge of others who are carrying out a task

overwhelm to defeat, beat down, or swallow up

oxygen very common gas that is one of the basic elements necessary for human and animal life

pagan (adjective) non-religious; *especially*, used disapprovingly to describe a form of worship very different from a familiar and socially acceptable religion

pagoda tower-like Asian temple or memorial building several storeys tall, with the edges of the roof at each level curving upwards

papyrus tall reed plant that grows in the Nile valley and that the ancient Egyptians used to make an early kind of paper

paraffin fuel for lanterns

paralyse to make someone or something unable to move

parasite creature that lives on another, which it usually injures

parka hooded heavy jacket for very cold weather

parliament the law-making body of some governments

particle tiny bit or piece

pastel type of drawing crayon

patent (verb) to legally protect the rights to make, use, or sell an invention; (noun) document that legally protects the ownership and use of an invention

patron saint holy person who is chosen to specially protect a group or place

peccary American animal related to the pig

peninsula a finger of land with water on three sides

perfection state of being without flaw or error

permanent unchanging, long-lasting, or meant to last forever

persecute (noun: **persecution**) to treat cruelly or harmfully for an extended period of time; *especially*, to make a person or group suffer because of their beliefs

pesticide poison that kills insects dangerous to growing plants

petroleum liquid taken from the ground and not yet cleaned or separated into such products as petrol and paraffin; also called 'crude oil'

philharmonic large orchestra that plays classical music

philosopher thinker or seeker after truth and understanding of basic concepts

photoelectric effect electrical effect produced when light strikes a metal surface

physics the science that deals with matter and energy and the way they interact

piazza open place or area formed at the meeting of two or more streets, especially in an Italian town

pied (adjective) having blotches of two or more colours

pilgrim person who travels to a shrine or holy place to worship

pilgrimage journey made to a holy place to worship there

plantation large farming property, usually worked by resident labourers

plate in the Earth sciences, a large segment of the Earth's crust (outer layer) that is constantly in motion

plateau wide land area with a fairly level surface raised sharply above the land on at least one side

plaza open place or area formed at the meeting of two or more streets

pleated folded and laid over another part of some material, especially a piece of cloth

plot the main story of a work of literature

poet laureate poet honoured by a country or other region as its most outstanding poet

polar region area at or near the North Pole or South Pole

polio serious disease that may kill or permanently weaken or paralyse its victims

political having to do with creating and controlling a government

pollen (verb: **pollinate**) very fine dusty substance that comes from flowers; it is important in the reproduction of other plants

pollute (noun: **pollution**) to poison or make dirty, often with man-made waste

polo team sport played by hitting a wooden ball with mallets through goalposts while on horseback

pope the leader of the Roman Catholic church

population all the people living in a country or other specific area

populous having a large population

porcelain hard white ceramic ware (earthenware) used especially for making dishes

porridge soft food made by boiling grain meal or a vegetable in milk or water until it thickens

port protected harbour where ships dock to load or unload goods

porter person who carries baggage

portray to show by making a picture or by imitating; also, to act the part of a character in a play

potential possible

poultry birds reared for their eggs or meat

poverty the condition of being poor

preach to deliver a sermon; to urge to accept an idea or course of action

precious of great value or high price

predator (adjective: **predatory**) animal that lives by eating other animals

predict to foretell an event on the basis of study, experience, or reasoning

prehistoric having to do with times before written history

presence the strong and self-confident quality a person has that makes others focus on him or her

prey an animal eaten by another animal

prime minister the chief officer of the government in some countries

primitive ancient, or belonging to a very early stage of development

print (noun) work of art made by a process that allows more than one copy of an image to be made

prism piece of many-sided clear crystal

procession group of people moving along in an orderly, often ceremonial way

Promised Land in Judaism, the land of Canaan, which God promised to Abraham and Moses if the Hebrew people promised to worship only him

propeller a device that uses blades that fan outwards from a central hub to propel (move) a vehicle, such as a boat or an airplane

prophet a holy person who acts as a messenger between God and people; also, a gifted person with the ability to accurately predict future events

prosperous wealthy

prowl to creep about in a sneaky way, often while hunting

psalm a sacred song or poem used in worship; especially, one of the biblical poems collected in the Book of Psalms

pulp 1) in plants, the juicy fleshy part of a soft fruit; 2) in industry, a mashed-up pasty glop such as the plant material used in making paper

pygmy something very small for its kind

pyramid structure with a square base and four sloping triangle sides that meet in a point at the top

quay structure built along the bank of a waterway for use as a landing place

rabies serious disease of animals that is usually passed on through the bite of a sick (rabid) animal; its effects include extreme salivation, strange behaviour, and usually death

radiation energy sent out in the form of rays, waves, or particles

rainforest dense tropical woodland with a high yearly rainfall and very tall trees

ray beam

rebel person who fights against an existing power or way of doing things

recitation act of speaking or reading a piece of literature aloud

reclaim to change to a wanted condition

recycle to reuse, or to pass used or scrap material through various changes in order to create new useful products from it

reef raised length of rocks, coral, or sand at or near the surface of water

refined polished, complex, and advanced

refinery factory that treats crude petroleum and separates it into different parts

region (adjective: **regional**) general area; also, a specific district

reign the time during which a ruler is in power

remains (noun) parts that are left after time passes or some event occurs

repel to force away or resist

reptile major animal group that includes snakes, lizards, and other animals that usually have scales or bony plates

republic form of government in which citizens who are allowed to elect officials and representatives responsible for governing by law

research careful search and study

reserve area of land set apart for some special purpose; also (usually plural, **reserves**), money or valuable items kept in hand or set apart until needed

resort (noun) holiday centre

resurrection raising from the dead

revere to honour

revolt (verb) to rise up (often violently) against the power of a ruler or government

revolution (adjective: **revolutionary**) activity or movement designed to make changes in a situation

rhythm (adjective: **rhythmic**) regular pattern of sound

rind the usually hard or tough outer layer or 'skin' of a fruit or vegetable

ritual formal custom or ceremony, often religious

roam to travel or wander freely through a wide area

rodent major animal group that includes mice, squirrels, and other small gnawing animals

rotate (noun: **rotation**) to spin or turn

rubble confused mass of rough or broken things

rudder flat piece attached to the back of a boat or ship and used for steering

ruthless without pity

sabotage damage or destruction of property that interferes with an enemy's use of it

sacred holy

sacrifice (noun) valuable offering made to a god; *especially*, a human or animal victim killed on an altar

saga tale of historic or legendary figures and events of Norway and Iceland

salvation rescue from the power and effects of sin

samurai warrior class in Japan from about the 12th to the mid-19th century

sanctuary safe place

sap the liquid inside a plant

satellite natural or man-made object that circles another object - usually a planet

savage extremely violent

savannah hot, dry grassland with scattered trees

saw-toothed having an edge or outline like the teeth (cutting points) of a saw

scale in biology, one of the small, stiff, flat plates that form an outer covering on the body of some animals, especially fishes and reptiles

Scandinavia area in northern Europe that includes the countries of Denmark, Norway, and Sweden

scenic having to do with a pleasing view or natural landscape

scholar person who has done advanced study in a special area

scholarship award of money to help pay for a person's education

science fiction stories that deal with the effects of real or imagined science on society or individuals

score in films, the background music that goes with the pictures on the screen

scorpion animal of the arachnid class (which includes spiders) that has a long body and a narrow sectioned tail with a poisonous stinger at the tip

scour to scrub hard

sculpture three-dimensional artwork, usually shaped by carving, moulding, or welding

sea level the height of the surface of the sea midway between the average high and low tides

seaport port, harbour, or town reachable by seagoing ships

seclusion isolation or separation from others

secretariat department that handles an international or government organization

sedge plant group found in marshes and related to grasses and rushes

self-portrait picture of a person, usually showing the face, that is painted or drawn by the artist himself or herself

semi-desert area that is much like a desert but has more rainfall

senate official law-making group of some nations

sensitive easily affected

sepulchre place of burial

seraphim in Christianity, Islam, and Judaism, special angels who guard God's throne

shears cutting device similar to scissors but usually larger

shortage situation of need, or amount that is missing or isn't enough

shrine place where honour or worship is offered to a saint or deity

skyline outline of buildings or other large objects against the background of the sky

sleet frozen or partly frozen rain

slum crowded, dirty, run-down housing

smog dirty air, a word made by combining 'smoke' and 'fog' to describe how the air looks

snout long projecting nose, like that of a pig; also, the long front part of the head of some animals, such as alligators

solar having to do with the Sun

solitary alone

sonar method of locating objects (usually underwater) by sending out sound waves to be reflected back from the objects

sophisticated complicated or stylish

soprano the highest woman's singing voice; also, a person who sings in this voice

Soviet Union country of eastern Europe and northern Asia that existed from 1922 to 1991 and consisted of Russia and 14 other republics

space shuttle rocket-launched airplane-like vehicle that transports people to and from space

species group of living things that have certain characteristics in common and share a name

sphere ball or globe

splendour something very grand or beautiful

spool reel for winding lengths of materials such as tape, thread, or wire

spout tube, pipe, or hole through which liquid flows

square open place or area formed at the meeting of two or more streets

squid sea mollusc that has a long thin body with eight short arms and two usually longer tentacles

staff wooden walking stick

stalk plant's main stem

standard commonly accepted amount or number

starchy containing starch, a natural substance that is made by green plants and is part of many foods

stationary unmoving

steppe land that is dry, usually rather level, and covered with grass

Stone Age the oldest period in which human beings are known to have existed, characterized by the making of stone tools

storage space to keep or hold on to things

strait narrow channel connecting two large bodies of water

strike temporary stopping of normal activities in protest against an act or condition

sturdy physically strong and healthy

stylized simplified or made to suggest natural forms but not imitate them

submerge to put under water

suction holding onto something by sucking

sultan king or ruler, especially of a Muslim state

summit top or highest point

superior better than

superstition unproven belief usually based on a mistaken idea of how something is caused

supreme highest, best, and without limit

supreme court the highest court in a country or other specific official area

surgery a medical procedure or operation for treating a disease or condition

symbolize to stand for something else; *especially*, to stand for or suggest something that cannot itself be pictured or shown

synagogue Jewish house of worship

synthetic produced artificially

tableland broad flat area of high land

tallow the solid fat of cattle and sheep, used chiefly in making soap, margarine, and candles

tamarind tropical tree whose sharp-tasting fruit is used as a flavouring

tannery place where animal hides are turned into leather, especially by soaking in a tannin solution

tap (verb) to make a hole in something in order to remove the liquid inside

tapered little by little becoming smaller towards one end

tapestry heavy cloth that has designs or pictures woven into it and is often used as a wall hanging

tapir hoofed, long-snouted mammal of Malaysia and the Americas that is related to horses and rhinoceroses

technical having to do with the way a skilled individual handles the details of an art or craft

technique special way of doing something; *especially*, the way a skilled individual handles the details of an art or craft

technology scientific ideas and knowledge put to actual use in actions, machines, and processes

teeming crowded

telegraph device for sending coded messages over long distances by using electrical signals

temperament personality or usual mood

temperate having mild weather

temple building used for worship

tentacle long arm-like structure on certain animals, usually found sticking out near the head or mouth and used especially for feeling or grasping

terrace area of hillside that has been leveled off to allow farming on the land

territorial protective of a territory or home area

terrorist person who uses violence to try to reach political goals

text written work

textile cloth

texture the feel of a surface

thatch to cover the roof of a building with plant material such as straw

theme the main idea or subject of a work of art; *especially*, in music, the main melody that a piece of music builds on

theory in science, an idea or reasoned explanation for why things are as they are or why things happen as they do

thermal springs a source of hot water coming from underground

thorax the middle of the three main divisions of the body of an insect

three-dimensional having depth (or thickness), in addition to width and height

timber wood used for building or carpentry

tolerate to put up with; also, to be able to survive

tollhouse building or booth where a fee is collected for some permission (such as using a motorway)

tomb special building or room in which a dead person is buried

topknot short mound of hair worn on the top of the head

tourism business of encouraging travel to a specific location and of managing services for visitors (including lodging, transport, food, and activities)

tourist person who travels for pleasure

tractor heavy vehicle used to pull farm equipment

tradition custom; habit of belief or of living

traditional usual; well known because of custom or longtime use

train (verb) in gardening and farming, to direct the growth of a plant, usually by bending, trimming, and tying off

translation version of a written work that has been changed from its original language into another

transmitter device that sends messages or code

tribute gift, performance, or action meant to show appreciation, respect, or caring for someone or something

tropical having to do with the Earth's warmest and most humid (moist) climates

troupe company or group; *especially*, a working group of stage performers

truce temporary stop in fighting during a war or other violent conflict

tsar one of the emperors of Russia until 1917

tsunami huge ocean wave produced by an undersea earthquake or volcanic eruption

tuft 1) in plants, a small cluster of flexible leaves or fibres that are attached or close together at the base and free at the opposite end; 2) in animals, a short mound of fur

tundra treeless plain with spotty grasses mostly in extremely cold regions

turban head covering made of a long cloth wrapped around the head or around a close-fitting cap

turpentine oil used to dissolve or thin out paint and other substances

tusk long tooth that overhangs when the mouth is closed and serves for digging food or as a weapon

tutor privately hired teacher

twilight the light between the end of day and the beginning of night; also, the name for that time of day

typhoon major tropical storm that occurs in the Pacific Ocean and features high winds moving in circular patterns; in the Atlantic Ocean such storms are called 'hurricanes'

tyrant powerful and cruel ruler; also, someone who acts like a tyrant

unique very unusual or one-of-a-kind

unity oneness or harmony

universal present or occurring everywhere

values morals or ideals

vapour substance in the state of a gas (rather than a solid or liquid)

vast huge or spacious

vaudeville popular American form of entertainment from the 1890s to the 1930s, involving musical, dancing, comedy, magic, and other variety acts

vegetarian person or animal that does not eat meat

vehicle device or machine used to carry something

venom poison that comes from animals

veterinarian doctor who takes care of animals

vibrate to move rapidly back and forth or from side to side

vivid bright or dramatic

vow solemn promise or statement

vulnerable exposed or in danger

wages payment for work or services

warm-blooded having a body temperature that stays mostly unchanged and is not affected by the surrounding environment

waste materials that are unused or left over after some work or action is finished

water power energy produced by moving water that can be used to do physical work; it may come directly from water's own force or from machines run by water that in turn produce even greater power (such as electricity)

waterlogged filled or soaked with water and therefore heavy or hard to manage

waterproof not affected by water

weaned capable of and used to eating food rather than nursing

weld to join metal parts together with heat

wildlife manager scientist who watches over the conditions, habitats, and populations of wild animals and plants

wildlife sanctuary place of protection for animals and plants

worship (verb) to honour and show surrender and obedience to a god or supernatural power

yacht small ship or large boat used for pleasure cruising or racing

What is an index?

An index is a guide to the many subjects in a book or a set of books. It tells you where to find each discussion of every subject.

Why do we use an index?

There is usually a table of contents at the beginning of a book. It tells you the major parts of the book, in order, and the page numbers where each section starts. But it doesn't tell you all the subjects that the book discusses or where to find them. For that, you need to use the index.

How do we use an index?

An index lists all the subjects of a book from A to Z. This makes it easy for you to find what you're looking for, as in the example below:

MY FIRST BRITANNICA
Index

Ando Hiroshige
(Japanese artist)
look under
Hiroshige

ants

apes

Arafat, Yasir
(Palestinian leader)

architecture

Argentina (country)

Armstrong, Louis
(American musician)

Ashoka (emperor of India)

Asia (continent)

astronauts, *also called*
cosmonauts (space explorers)

Notice that the subjects are in **bold-faced type** and in alphabetical order. Notice, also, several other clues that will help you use the index.

First, many subjects

are followed by a word or phrase in parentheses that describes the subject.

Second, people

with last names have their last names listed first. **Armstrong, Louis** is one example. **Ashoka** is an example of a person without a last name. He is therefore listed under this single name.

Third, some

subjects, such as **Ando Hiroshige**, are known by more than one name. In such cases, the index may tell you to look under a different name. All the names of a subject are also included with the name the index tells you to look under. They follow the words *also called.* For example, you'll find the subject **cosmonauts** in **bold-faced type** with an instruction to *look under* astronauts:

cosmonauts (space explorers): *look under* astronauts

Then at **astronauts** you'll find:

astronauts, *also called* cosmonauts (space explorers)

Some subjects are discussed only in articles on other topics. To find them, the index tells you to *look under* related subjects. For example:

moons (satellites of planets): *look under* Moon; *for other moons look under the planets* Jupiter; Mars; Neptune; Pluto; Saturn; Uranus

© Kennan Ward/Corbis

Mountain gorilla.

So the first things you need to do to find a subject in the index are:

1 Choose a word or phrase that best describes the subject you're interested in. Subjects can be things such as **music** or **telescopes**, places such as **Rome** or **Tokyo**, or people such as **Judi Dench** or **Albert Einstein**. (Remember to look under the last name for most people.)

2 If you can't find the subject you're looking for in the alphabetical list, try to think of different words for your subject and look again. For example, you may want to know about maps. You'll find the information under **atlas**.

3 Once you locate your subject in the index, you'll see that the index works like a map. At each subject, you'll find explanations of how to get to all the places that discuss or illustrate your subject.

How to

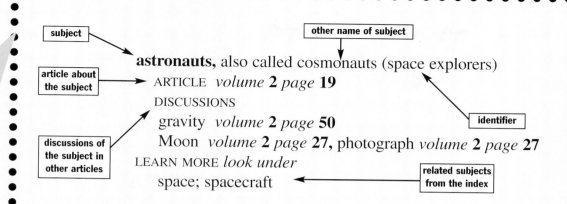

subject

other name of subject

astronauts, also called cosmonauts (space explorers)

article about the subject → ARTICLE *volume* **2** *page* **19**

DISCUSSIONS

discussions of the subject in other articles

gravity *volume* **2** *page* **50**

Moon *volume* **2** *page* **27**, photograph *volume* **2** *page* **27**

identifier

LEARN MORE *look under*

space; spacecraft

related subjects from the index

Space shuttle *Endeavor*.

© NASA

There are important things to notice in this example. If there is an entire article written about your subject, you'll see the word ARTICLE followed by the *volume* and *page* numbers where it can be found:

ARTICLE *volume* **2** *page* **19**

If your subject is also discussed or illustrated in articles other than the main article, or if it appears on a map in the mini-atlas in Volume 13, you'll see the word DISCUSSIONS. Below this is a word or phrase describing each of the other articles or indicating the mini-atlas, also followed by the *volume* and *page* numbers where each can be found. If there are also photographs or illustrations related to your subject, they too will be listed along with their *volume* and *page* numbers:

DISCUSSIONS

gravity *volume* **2** *page* **50**

Moon *volume* **2** *page* **27**, photograph *volume* **2** *page* **27**

Sometimes you'll see the phrase Did you know? followed by a *volume* and a *page* number. This means that you'll find information about your subject in the DID YOU KNOW? box on that page.

The index sometimes helps you learn more about your subject by giving you a list of related subjects. You'll find these after the words LEARN MORE *look under*

LEARN MORE *look under* space; spacecraft

Earth's Moon.
© Jet Propulsion Laboratory/NASA

Now you're ready to explore MY FIRST BRITANNICA, **using one of the best guides there is - the index!**

use the index

African manatees (mammals)
DISCUSSIONS
manatees *volume* **12** *page* **73**

African National Congress, *also called* ANC (South African political party)
DISCUSSIONS
Nelson Mandela *volume* **4** *page* **53**

agriculture: *look under* farming

ahimsa (religion)
DISCUSSIONS
Hinduism *volume* **5** *page* **79**
Jainism *volume* **5** *page* **87**
LEARN MORE *look under* non-violence

Ahriman (evil spirit)
DISCUSSIONS
Zoroastrianism *volume* **5** *page* **49**

Ahura Mazda, *also called* Ormazd (god)
DISCUSSIONS
Zoroastrianism *volume* **5** *page* **49**
LEARN MORE *look under* God

'Aida' (opera by Verdi)
DISCUSSIONS
opera photograph *volume* **3** *page* **76**

Aigams (city in Namibia): *look under* Windhoek

Ailey, Alvin (American dance artist)
ARTICLE *volume* **3** *page* **78**
LEARN MORE *look under*
other dancers: Elssler, Fanny; Tallchief, Maria
other famous African Americans: Armstrong, Louis; Basie, Count; Brooks, Gwendolyn

air
DISCUSSIONS
dew *volume* **1** *page* **65**
LEARN MORE *look under* clouds; cyclones; echoes; northern lights; rainbows; thunder and lightning; wind power

aircraft: *look under* airplanes; ballooning; helicopters; space shuttles

airplanes, *also called* aeroplanes
ARTICLE *volume* **2** *page* **71**
DISCUSSIONS
seaplane over the ocean photograph *volume* **7** *page* **93**
LEARN MORE *look under* transportation

Aklavik (town in Canada)
ARTICLE *volume* **9** *page* **13**
LEARN MORE *look under* Canada

Alaska (state in the U.S.)
DISCUSSIONS
atlas *volume* **13** *page* **14**
Did you know? *volume* **2** *page* **84**
glaciers photograph *volume* **1** *page* **55**
peninsulas *volume* **1** *page* **22**
pines photograph *volume* **10** *page* **88**
sheep photograph *volume* **12** *page* **57**
United States of America *volume* **9** *page* **27**
LEARN MORE *look under* United States of America

albatrosses (birds)
ARTICLE *volume* **11** *page* **17**
LEARN MORE *look under* birds; marine animals

Aldrin, Edwin E., *also called* Buzz Aldrin (American astronaut)
DISCUSSIONS
walking on the Moon photograph *volume* **2** *page* **27**

Aleutian Islands (U.S.)
DISCUSSIONS
islands *volume* **1** *page* **12**

Algeria (country)
ARTICLE *volume* **8** *page* **44**
DISCUSSIONS
atlas *volume* **13** *page* **12**
flag *volume* **8** *page* **44**
LEARN MORE *look under*
places: Algiers; North Africa

Algiers (city in Algeria)
ARTICLE *volume* **8** *page* **47**
DISCUSSIONS
atlas *volume* **13** *page* **12**
LEARN MORE *look under* Algeria

'Alice's Adventures in Wonderland' (book by Carroll)
DISCUSSIONS
Lewis Carroll *volume* **3** *page* **59**, photograph *volume* **3** *page* **58**

All Souls' Day, *also called* Dia de los Muertos (holiday)
DISCUSSIONS
Mexico *volume* **9** *page* **41**

Allah (name for God)
DISCUSSIONS
Islam *volume* **5** *page* **64**
Koran *volume* **5** *page* **69**
Muhammad *volume* **5** *page* **67**
LEARN MORE *look under* God

Allende, Isabel (Chilean writer)
ARTICLE *volume* **4** *page* **7**
LEARN MORE *look under* Chile; Latin America; literature

alligators and crocodiles
ARTICLE *volume* **11** *page* **77**
LEARN MORE *look under* aquatic animals; hippopotamuses; reptiles; rivers

alpacas (mammals)
DISCUSSIONS
Did you know? *volume* **9** *page* **75**
LEARN MORE *look under* ungulates

Alpha Proxima Centuri (star)
DISCUSSIONS
Did you know? *volume* **2** *page* **10**

Alps (mountains in Europe)
DISCUSSIONS
atlas *volume* **13** *page* **6**
Austria *volume* **6** *page* **48**
Italy *volume* **6** *page* **89**
Switzerland *volume* **6** *page* **46**, photograph *volume* **6** *page* **47**
LEARN MORE *look under* Blanc, Mont; Central Europe; mountains

Alvin Ailey American Dance Theater
DISCUSSIONS
Alvin Ailey *volume* **3** *page* **78**

Amaterasu (Shinto goddess)
DISCUSSIONS
Did you know? *volume* **5** *page* **77**
LEARN MORE *look under* God

Amazon (river and region in South America)
ARTICLE *volume* **9** *page* **62**
DISCUSSIONS
atlas photograph *volume* **13** *page* **16**
anacondas *volume* **11** *page* **81**
Brazil *volume* **9** *page* **79**
Did you know? *volume* **10** *page* **15**
marshes *volume* **1** *page* **26**
Peru *volume* **9** *page* **75**
piranhas *volume* **11** *page* **41**
rivers *volume* **1** *page* **31**, *volume* **9** *page* **64**
South America *volume* **9** *page* **61**
swamps *volume* **1** *page* **28**
LEARN MORE *look under* rainforests; rivers
animals: anacondas; ants; butterflies and moths; crocodiles; manatees; monkeys; parrots and cockatoos; piranhas; spiders

Amazon parrot
DISCUSSIONS
Amazon photograph *volume* **9** *page* **65**
LEARN MORE *look under* birds

stories: fables; folktales; legends; myths

Annan, Kofi (Ghanaian and United Nations leader)
DISCUSSIONS
Jane Goodall photograph *volume* **4** *page* **78**

'Annie Allen' (book by Brooks)
DISCUSSIONS
Gwendolyn Brooks *volume* **3** *page* **56**

anoa (animals)
DISCUSSIONS
buffalo *volume* **12** *page* **49**

anoles, *also called* false chameleons (lizards)
DISCUSSIONS
chameleons *volume* **11** *page* **87**

ant hills
DISCUSSIONS
ants *volume* **11** *page* **59**

Antarctica (continent)
ARTICLE *volume* **1** *page* **10**
DISCUSSIONS
atlas *volume* **13** *page* **19**
continents *volume* **1** *page* **8,** map *volume* **1** *page* **8**
Did you know? *volume* **2** *page* **42**
LEARN MORE *look under* glaciers; icebergs
animals: albatrosses; penguins

antelope (animals): *look under* gazelles

antennae, *also called* antennas
DISCUSSIONS
ants *volume* **11** *page* **59**

antibiotics (medicines)
DISCUSSIONS
medicine *volume* **2** *page* **60**

Antony, Mark (Roman official)
DISCUSSIONS
Cleopatra *volume* **4** *page* **43**

ants
ARTICLE *volume* **11** *page* **59**
DISCUSSIONS
Did you know? *volume* **11** *page* **6**
LEARN MORE *look under* insects

Anubis (Egyptian god)
DISCUSSIONS
Did you know? *volume* **12** *page* **29**
LEARN MORE *look under* God

apartheid (racial segregation in South Africa)

DISCUSSIONS
South Africa *volume* **8** *page* **85,** photograph *volume* **8** *page* **85**

apatosaurs, *also called* brontosaurs (dinosaurs)
DISCUSSIONS
dinosaurs *volume* **1** *page* **88**

apes
ARTICLE *volume* **12** *page* **9**
LEARN MORE *look under*
kinds of apes: chimpanzees; gibbons; gorillas
similar animals: lemurs; monkeys

aphids (animals)
DISCUSSIONS
ants *volume* **11** *page* **59**

Appalachian Mountains
DISCUSSIONS
atlas *volume* **13** *page* **14**
mountains *volume* **1** *page* **16**
LEARN MORE *look under* mountains

apples (fruit)
ARTICLE *volume* **10** *page* **41**
LEARN MORE *look under* fruits and vegetables; trees

aquatic animals: *look under* alligators and crocodiles; dolphins; ducks; fish; geese; hippopotamuses; marine animals; muskrats; platypuses; swans

Arabia (peninsula and region in Asia)
DISCUSSIONS
atlas *volume* **13** *page* **8**
peninsulas *volume* **1** *page* **22**
LEARN MORE *look under*
people: Arabs
places: Baghdad; Mecca; Middle East; Oman
religion: Islam
animals: camels; wild goats

Arabian camels (animals): *look under* dromedaries

'Arabian Nights' (collection of stories)
DISCUSSIONS
Baghdad *volume* **7** *page* **73**

Arabs (people)
DISCUSSIONS
Abraham *volume* **5** *page* **53**
Israel *volume* **7** *page* **75**
Menachem Begin *volume* **4** *page* **35**
LEARN MORE *look under*
places: Arabia; Middle East; North Africa
religion: Islam
people: peoples

arachnids (animals)
DISCUSSIONS
spiders *volume* **11** *page* **72**
LEARN MORE *look under* insects

Arafat, Yasir (Palestinian leader)
ARTICLE *volume* **4** *page* **30**
LEARN MORE *look under* Middle East
other Middle Eastern leaders: Begin, Menachem; Meir, Golda; Sadat, Anwar el-

Ararat, Mount (mountain in Turkey)
DISCUSSIONS
Yerevan *volume* **7** *page* **67**

Arawak (people)
DISCUSSIONS
Puerto Rico *volume* **9** *page* **57**
LEARN MORE *look under* peoples

architecture
ARTICLE *volume* **3** *page* **13**
LEARN MORE *look under*
people: Costa, Lucio; Fathy, Hassan; Michelangelo; Pei, I. M.
buildings and constructions: Acropolis; Angkor Wat; Barracks Arch; Brandenburg Gate; bridges; castles; Colosseum; dams; Dionysus, Theatre of; Dome of the Rock; dzong; Empire State Building; Eurotunnel; Fushimi Inari shrine; Gateway Arch; Great Wall; Jefferson Memorial; Machu Picchu; mosques; palaces; Panama Canal; Parliament House; pyramids; Sadat Resthouse; Sarnath; Stonehenge; Suez Canal; Taj Mahal; temples; totem pole; towers; Western Wall

Arctic Ocean: *look under*
animals: walruses

Argentina (country)
ARTICLE *volume* **9** *page* **90**
DISCUSSIONS
atlas *volume* **13** *page* **17**
flag *volume* **9** *page* **90**
LEARN MORE *look under*
people: Borges, Jorge Luis
places: Buenos Aires; South America

Arizona (state in the U.S.)
DISCUSSIONS
Grand Canyon *volume* **9** *page* **32,** photograph *volume* **9** *page* **33**
LEARN MORE *look under* United States of America

Arjumand Banu Baygam (Mughal queen): *look under* Mumtaz Mahal

Bahubali (Jainism)
DISCUSSIONS
Jainism photograph *volume* **5** *page* **87**

Baikal, Lake (lake in Russia)
DISCUSSIONS
atlas *volume* **13** *page* **8**
Russia *volume* **6** *page* **69**
LEARN MORE *look under* lakes

Balanchine, George
(Russian-American choreographer)
DISCUSSIONS
Maria Tallchief *volume* **3** *page* **91**
LEARN MORE *look under* ballet

bald cypress (trees)
DISCUSSIONS
swamps photograph *volume* **1** *page* **29**
LEARN MORE *look under* trees

bald eagles (birds)
DISCUSSIONS
eagles *volume* **11** *page* **14**,
photograph *volume* **11** *page* **15**

baleen (skin)
DISCUSSIONS
whales *volume* **12** *page* **77**

Bali (island and province in Indonesia)
DISCUSSIONS
dance photograph *volume* **3** *page* **70**
LEARN MORE *look under* Indonesia

ballet (dance)
DISCUSSIONS
dance *volume* **3** *page* **70**
LEARN MORE *look under*
people: Ailey, Alvin; Elssler, Fanny;
Tallchief, Maria

ballooning (flying)
DISCUSSIONS
Did you know? *volume* **2** *page* **65**
LEARN MORE *look under* aircraft

bamboo (plants)
ARTICLE *volume* **10** *page* **67**
DISCUSSIONS
pandas *volume* **12** *page* **38**
LEARN MORE *look under* grasses

bananas
ARTICLE *volume* **10** *page* **21**
LEARN MORE *look under* fruits and
vegetables

Bandaranaike, Sirimavo R. D. (Sri
Lankan leader)
DISCUSSIONS
Did you know? *volume* **4** *page* **57**
LEARN MORE *look under* Sri Lanka

Banff National Park (park in Canada)
DISCUSSIONS
Canada photograph *volume* **9** *page* **11**

Bangkok, *also called* Krung Thep (city
in Thailand)
ARTICLE *volume* **7** *page* **39**
DISCUSSIONS
atlas *volume* **13** *page* **8**
LEARN MORE *look under* Southeast
Asia; Thailand

Bangladesh (country)
ARTICLE *volume* **7** *page* **47**
DISCUSSIONS
atlas *volume* **13** *page* **8**
flag *volume* **7** *page* **47**
Rabindranath Tagore *volume* **3**
page **67**
LEARN MORE *look under*
animals: Bengal tigers
places: India; Pakistan; South Asia
religions: Hinduism; Islam

Bangladesh, the Concert for
DISCUSSIONS
Ravi Shankar photograph *volume* **3**
page **49**

Bar Mitzvah (religion)
DISCUSSIONS
Judaism *volume* **5** *page* **50**,
photograph *volume* **5** *page* **51**
LEARN MORE *look under* navjote

'Barber of Seville, The' (opera by
Rossini)
DISCUSSIONS
opera *volume* **3** *page* **76**

barley (grain)
ARTICLE *volume* **10** *page* **69**
LEARN MORE *look under* grasses

barn owls (birds)
DISCUSSIONS
owls photograph *volume* **11** *page* **12**

Barracks Arch (structure in Perth,
Australia)
DISCUSSIONS
Western Australia photograph
volume **7** *page* **96**
LEARN MORE *look under* architecture;
Australia

Bas Mitzvah (religion): *look under* Bat
Mitzvah

baseball (sport)
DISCUSSIONS
Did you know? *volume* **4** *page* **38**,
volume **9** *page* **49**
LEARN MORE *look under* sports

Basho, *also called* Matsuo Munefusa
(Japanese poet)
ARTICLE *volume* **3** *page* **52**
LEARN MORE *look under* literature
people: Brooks, Gwendolyn;
Dickinson, Emily; Hiroshige;
Kurosawa, Akira; Tagore,
Rabindranath; Walker, Kath
places: Japan
things: Buddhism

Basie, Count, *also called* William Basie
(American musician)
ARTICLE *volume* **4** *page* **9**
LEARN MORE *look under* jazz
other famous African Americans: Ailey,
Alvin; Armstrong, Louis; Brooks,
Gwendolyn

Bat Mitzvah, *also called* Bas Mitzvah
(religion)
DISCUSSIONS
Judaism *volume* **5** *page* **50**

Batista, Fulgencio (Cuban leader)
DISCUSSIONS
Fidel Castro *volume* **4** *page* **39**

Batlle, Jorge (Uruguayan leader)
DISCUSSIONS
Jorge Luis Borges photograph
volume **3** *page* **54**

bats (animals)
ARTICLE *volume* **12** *page* **89**
DISCUSSIONS
echoes *volume* **1** *page* **69**
LEARN MORE *look under* birds;
mammals

Batswana (people): *look under* Tswana

battery (electricity)
DISCUSSIONS
energy *volume* **2** *page* **48**

bazaars (markets)
DISCUSSIONS
Algiers photograph *volume* **8** *page* **46**
Amman *volume* **7** *page* **79**
Damascus *volume* **7** *page* **87**

BBC: *look under* British Broadcasting
Corporation

bearded pigs
DISCUSSIONS
pigs *volume* **12** *page* **64**

bears (animals): *look under* pandas;
polar bears

Beatles, the (British rock group)
DISCUSSIONS
Did you know? *volume* **3** *page* **33**
Ravi Shankar *volume* **3** *page* **48**

LEARN MORE *look under* popular music

Becquerel, Henri (French scientist)
DISCUSSIONS
Marie Curie *volume* **4** *page* **71**

bee bread
DISCUSSIONS
bees *volume* **11** *page* **61**

beehive
DISCUSSIONS
bees *volume* **11** *page* **61**

bees (insects)
ARTICLE *volume* **11** *page* **61**
LEARN MORE *look under* insects

Beethoven, Ludwig van (German composer)
ARTICLE *volume* **3** *page* **40**
LEARN MORE *look under* classical music
people: Mozart, Wolfgang Amadeus

Begin, Menachem (Israeli leader)
ARTICLE *volume* **4** *page* **35**
DISCUSSIONS
Anwar el-Sadat *volume* **4** *page* **59**
LEARN MORE *look under* Israel
other Middle Eastern leaders: Arafat, Yasir; Meir, Golda

Beihai Park (park in Beijing, China)
DISCUSSIONS
Beijing *volume* **7** *page* **11**

Beijing, *also called* Peking (city in China)
ARTICLE *volume* **7** *page* **11**
DISCUSSIONS
atlas *volume* **13** *page* **8**
LEARN MORE *look under* China

Beijing Zoo, *also called* Garden of Ten Thousand Animals (zoo in Beijing, China)
DISCUSSIONS
Beijing *volume* **7** *page* **11**

Beirut (city in Lebanon)
ARTICLE *volume* **7** *page* **80**
DISCUSSIONS
atlas *volume* **13** *page* **8**
LEARN MORE *look under* Lebanon; Middle East

Belfast (city in Northern Ireland, U.K.)
DISCUSSIONS
atlas *volume* **13** *page* **6**
Ireland *volume* **6** *page* **24**
LEARN MORE *look under* United Kingdom

Belgium (country)
DISCUSSIONS
atlas *volume* **13** *page* **6**

flag *volume* **6** *page* **36**
LEARN MORE *look under*
places: Brussels; Western Europe

Belgrade, *also called* Beograd (city in Serbia and Montenegro)
ARTICLE *volume* **6** *page* **79**
DISCUSSIONS
atlas *volume* **13** *page* **6**
LEARN MORE *look under* Serbia and Montenegro

Belize (country)
DISCUSSIONS
Central America *volume* **9** *page* **45**

Bell, Alexander Graham (American inventor)
DISCUSSIONS
Helen Keller *volume* **4** *page* **97**
telephones *volume* **2** *page* **100**

bell peppers (plants)
DISCUSSIONS
peppers *volume* **10** *page* **34,** photograph *volume* **10** *page* **35**
LEARN MORE *look under* fruits and vegetables

belted kingfishers (birds)
DISCUSSIONS
kingfishers *volume* **11** *page* **9**
LEARN MORE *look under* birds

beluga whales
DISCUSSIONS
whales photograph *volume* **12** *page* **76**
LEARN MORE *look under* marine animals

Bengal tigers
DISCUSSIONS
tigers *volume* **12** *page* **23,** photograph *volume* **12** *page* **22**
LEARN MORE *look under* cats
countries: Bangladesh; India

Beograd (city in Serbia and Montenegro): *look under* Belgrade

'Beowulf' (English story)
DISCUSSIONS
Did you know? *volume* **6** *page* **14**

Berbers (people)
DISCUSSIONS
Libya *volume* **8** *page* **58**
LEARN MORE *look under* peoples

Berlin (city in Germany)
ARTICLE *volume* **6** *page* **45**
DISCUSSIONS
atlas *volume* **13** *page* **6**
Germany *volume* **6** *page* **43**

LEARN MORE *look under* Germany

Berlin Wall
DISCUSSIONS
Berlin *volume* **6** *page* **45,** photograph *volume* **6** *page* **44**
Germany *volume* **6** *page* **43**

Bernhardt, Sarah, *also called* The Divine Sarah (French actress)
ARTICLE *volume* **3** *page* **81**
LEARN MORE *look under* theatre
people: Dench, Judi; Welles, Orson

berserkers (warriors)
DISCUSSIONS
Did you know? *volume* **4** *page* **63**

Bhutan (country)
DISCUSSIONS
atlas *volume* **13** *page* **8**
flag *volume* **7** *page* **49**
LEARN MORE *look under*
places: Thimphu
animals: yaks

Bible (holy book)
ARTICLE *volume* **5** *page* **63**
DISCUSSIONS
Did you know? *volume* **5** *page* **54**
Jesus Christ *volume* **5** *page* **58**
Mary *volume* **5** *page* **61**
myths *volume* **5** *page* **7**
printing *volume* **2** *page* **90**
LEARN MORE *look under*
people: Abraham; Jesus Christ; Mary; Moses
religions: Christianity; Judaism
similar writings: Koran

bicycling (sport): *look under* cycling

Bidpai (South Asian stories)
DISCUSSIONS
Kalilah wa Dimnah *volume* **5** *page* **18**

big-band music
DISCUSSIONS
jazz *volume* **3** *page* **35**
popular music *volume* **3** *page* **32**

big bang theory (science)
DISCUSSIONS
universe *volume* **2** *page* **8**
LEARN MORE *look under* astronomy

Big Ben (clock tower in London, England, U.K.)
DISCUSSIONS
London *volume* **6** *page* **16,** photograph *volume* **6** *page* **17**

bioluminescence (light)
DISCUSSIONS
deep-sea life *volume* **11** *page* **54**

crows (birds): *look under*
stories: 'How Crow Brought Daylight to the World'

Crusades (Christianity)
DISCUSSIONS
religion *volume* **5** *page* **42**

Cuba (country)
ARTICLE *volume* **9** *page* **59**
DISCUSSIONS
atlas *volume* **13** *page* **14**
flag *volume* **9** *page* **59**
LEARN MORE *look under*
people: Castro, Fidel
places: West Indies
things: sugarcane

Cubism (art)
DISCUSSIONS
Pablo Picasso *volume* **4** *page* **20**
LEARN MORE *look under* painting

culture: *look under* civilizations

cumulonimbus clouds, *also called* thunderclouds
DISCUSSIONS
clouds *volume* **1** *page* **56**
thunder and lightning *volume* **1** *page* **58**
LEARN MORE *look under* weather

cumulus clouds
DISCUSSIONS
clouds *volume* **1** *page* **56**
LEARN MORE *look under* weather

curare (drug)
DISCUSSIONS
medicine *volume* **2** *page* **60**
rainforests *volume* **1** *page* **24**

Curie, Marie (French scientist)
ARTICLE *volume* **4** *page* **71**
LEARN MORE *look under*
people: Pasteur, Louis
things: atoms; medicine; nuclear energy; science

Curie, Pierre (French scientist)
DISCUSSIONS
Marie Curie *volume* **4** *page* **71**

currents
DISCUSSIONS
Atlantic Ocean *volume* **1** *page* **39**
Did you know? *volume* **6** *page* **64**
oceans *volume* **1** *page* **37**

Curtiss, Glenn (American bicycle maker)
DISCUSSIONS
airplanes *volume* **2** *page* **71**

cycling, *also called* bicycling (sport)
DISCUSSIONS
Did you know? *volume* **1** *page* **55**, *volume* **2** *page* **49**
Beijing photograph *volume* **7** *page* **10**
LEARN MORE *look under* sports

cyclones, *also called* hurricanes, *or* typhoons (wind storms)
ARTICLE *volume* **1** *page* **61**
DISCUSSIONS
floods *volume* **1** *page* **32**
waves *volume* **1** *page* **49**
LEARN MORE *look under* weather

Cyclopes (legendary giants)
DISCUSSIONS
legend of Odysseus *volume* **5** *page* **27**
LEARN MORE *look under* legends

cygnets (birds)
DISCUSSIONS
swans *volume* **11** *page* **24**, photograph *volume* **11** *page* **24**, photograph *volume* **11** *page* **25**

Cymru (country in the U.K.): *look under* Wales

Czech Republic (country)
ARTICLE *volume* **6** *page* **52**
DISCUSSIONS
atlas *volume* **13** *page* **6**
flag *volume* **6** *page* **52**
LEARN MORE *look under*
places: Central Europe; Prague

Czechoslovakia (historic nation in Europe)
DISCUSSIONS
Czech Republic *volume* **6** *page* **52**

dabbling ducks (birds)
DISCUSSIONS
ducks *volume* **11** *page* **21**

daisies (plants)
DISCUSSIONS
Luther Burbank *volume* **4** *page* **66**

Dakar (city in Senegal)
ARTICLE *volume* **8** *page* **25**
DISCUSSIONS
atlas *volume* **13** *page* **12**
Senegal *volume* **8** *page* **23**
LEARN MORE *look under* West Africa

Dalai Lama (Tibetan leader)
ARTICLE *volume* **5** *page* **85**
LEARN MORE *look under* Buddhism; monasticism

Dall's sheep
DISCUSSIONS
sheep photograph *volume* **12** *page* **57**

Damascus (city in Syria)
ARTICLE *volume* **7** *page* **87**
DISCUSSIONS
atlas *volume* **13** *page* **8**
LEARN MORE *look under* Syria

dams
DISCUSSIONS
water power *volume* **2** *page* **67**, illustration *volume* **2** *page* **66**
LEARN MORE *look under* dykes
dams: Aswan High Dam; Kariba Dam

dance
ARTICLE *volume* **3** *page* **70**
DISCUSSIONS
Did you know? *volume* **5** *page* **90**
LEARN MORE *look under*
people: Ailey, Alvin; Elssler, Fanny; Tallchief, Maria

Danube, *also called* Blue Danube (river in Europe)
DISCUSSIONS
atlas *volume* **13** *page* **6**
Austria *volume* **6** *page* **48**
Budapest *volume* **6** *page* **70**, photograph *volume* **6** *page* **71**
Did you know? *volume* **6** *page* **78**
LEARN MORE *look under* rivers
places: Bucharest; Vienna

Dao, *also called* Tao (Chinese philosophy)
DISCUSSIONS
Daoism *volume* **5** *page* **74**

'Daodejing' (Daoism)
DISCUSSIONS
Daoism *volume* **5** *page* **74**
LEARN MORE *look under*
other holy books: 'Adi Granth'; Avesta; Bible; Koran

Daoism, *also called* Taoism (religion and philosophy)
ARTICLE *volume* **5** *page* **74**
DISCUSSIONS
Shinto *volume* **5** *page* **77**
LEARN MORE *look under* Buddhism; Confucius

DISCUSSIONS

Did you know? *volume* **9** *page* **7,** *volume* **9** *page* **61**

disappearance *volume* **1** *page* **91**

dragons *volume* **5** *page* **9**

LEARN MORE *look under* chalk; fossils; mammoths and mastodons; reptiles; tyrannosaurs

Dionysus, Theatre of (Athens, Greece)

DISCUSSIONS

Athens *volume* **6** *page* **85,** photograph *volume* **6** *page* **84**

LEARN MORE *look under* architecture; theatre

directing (arts)

DISCUSSIONS

motion pictures *volume* **2** *page* **83**

theatre *volume* **3** *page* **72**

LEARN MORE *look under* Ray, Satyajit

disasters: *look under* cyclones; earthquakes; floods; tsunamis; volcanoes

diseases: *look under* medicine; Pasteur, Louis

Divine Sarah, The (French actress): *look under* Bernhardt, Sarah

diving bells (spiders)

DISCUSSIONS

spiders *volume* **11** *page* **73**

diving ducks (birds)

DISCUSSIONS

ducks *volume* **11** *page* **21**

Dixieland (music)

DISCUSSIONS

jazz *volume* **3** *page* **35**

Dodgson, Charles (British writer): *look under* Carroll, Lewis

dogs

ARTICLE *volume* **12** *page* **29**

DISCUSSIONS

Did you know? *volume* **5** *page* **47**

sheep *volume* **12** *page* **57**

LEARN MORE *look under* carnivores *similar animals:* coyotes; wolves *other pets:* cats *stories and characters:* Aesop's fables; Pluto

dolls

DISCUSSIONS

kachina dolls photograph *volume* **3** *page* **7**

dolphins (animals)

DISCUSSIONS

Did you know? *volume* **12** *page* **7,** *volume* **12** *page* **8,** photograph *volume* **12** *page* **6**

LEARN MORE *look under* aquatic animals; manatees; marine animals; walruses; whales

Dome of the Rock (shrine in Jerusalem, Israel)

DISCUSSIONS

Islam photograph *volume* **5** *page* **64**

Jerusalem *volume* **7** *page* **77,** photograph *volume* **7** *page* **76**

LEARN MORE *look under* architecture

domestic cats: *look under* cats

domesticated animals: *look under* buffalo; camels; cats; cattle; dogs; donkeys; elephants; horses; llamas; pigs; sheep; yaks

Donatello (Italian sculptor)

DISCUSSIONS

sculpture photograph *volume* **3** *page* **11**

LEARN MORE *look under* Michelangelo; Picasso, Pablo; Rodin, Auguste

Dong Kinh (city in Vietnam): *look under* Hanoi

donkeys, *also called* burros (animals)

ARTICLE *volume* **12** *page* **42**

LEARN MORE *look under* horses; ungulates

double coconut trees: *look under* coco de mer

Dover (city in England, U.K.)

DISCUSSIONS

English Channel photograph *volume* **6** *page* **30**

LEARN MORE *look under* White Cliffs of Dover

down (feathers)

DISCUSSIONS

geese *volume* **11** *page* **22**

LEARN MORE *look under* feathers

draco lizards

DISCUSSIONS

lizards *volume* **11** *page* **85**

'Dracula' (book by Stoker)

DISCUSSIONS

Did you know? *volume* **6** *page* **72**

Dragon Lady, The (empress of China): *look under* Empress of China

dragon ships: *look under* longships

dragonflies (insects)

DISCUSSIONS

insects *volume* **11** *page* **57,** illustration *volume* **11** *page* **57**

dragons, *also called* long

ARTICLE *volume* **5** *page* **9**

LEARN MORE *look under* *other European stories:* Aesop's fables; Atlas; 'Golem of Prague, The'; Knights of the Round Table; 'Odysseus and the Cyclops'; Trojan Horse, The *other legends:* Bunyan, Paul

drama (literature and theatre)

DISCUSSIONS

Did you know? *volume* **5** *page* **90**

theatre *volume* **3** *page* **72**

dromedaries, *also called* Arabian camels (camels)

DISCUSSIONS

camels *volume* **12** *page* **60,** photograph *volume* **12** *page* **61**

drones (animals)

DISCUSSIONS

bees *volume* **11** *page* **61**

drugs: *look under* medicine

drums (musical instruments): *look under* percussion instruments; rhythm instruments

Dublin (city in Ireland)

ARTICLE *volume* **6** *page* **26**

DISCUSSIONS

atlas *volume* **13** *page* **6**

Ireland *volume* **6** *page* **24**

LEARN MORE *look under* Western Europe

duckbilled platypuses (animals): *look under* platypuses

ducks

ARTICLE *volume* **11** *page* **21**

DISCUSSIONS

Did you know? *volume* **1** *page* **68**

LEARN MORE *look under* birds

Dun Eideann (city in Scotland, U.K.): *look under* Edinburgh

Durbar Square (square in Kathmandu, Nepal)

DISCUSSIONS

Kathmandu photograph *volume* **7** *page* **56**

dykes (dams)

DISCUSSIONS

Netherlands, the *volume* **6** *page* **38**

LEARN MORE *look under* dams

dzong (building)
DISCUSSIONS
Thimphu *volume* **7** *page* **49**
LEARN MORE *look under* architecture

eagles (birds)
ARTICLE *volume* **11** *page* **14**
LEARN MORE *look under* birds

Earth (planet)
VOLUME **1**
DISCUSSIONS
calendars *volume* **2** *page* **77**
Did you know? *volume* **2** *page* **16**
solar system illustration *volume* **2** *page* **20**
LEARN MORE *look under* planets

Earth sciences: *look under* Earth; geography; geology

earthquakes
DISCUSSIONS
floods *volume* **1** *page* **32**
mountains *volume* **1** *page* **16**
tsunamis *volume* **1** *page* **50**
LEARN MORE *look under*
places: Japan

East Asia
DISCUSSIONS
painting *volume* **3** *page* **8**
LEARN MORE *look under*
places: Beijing; China; Great Wall; Japan; Korean Peninsula; Pyongyang; Seoul
religion: Buddhism; Confucianism; Daoism; Shinto
animals: pandas; tigers

East Indies (islands in Southeast Asia)
DISCUSSIONS
Ferdinand Magellan *volume* **4** *page* **101**
West Indies *volume* **9** *page* **54**

East Pakistan (historic region): *look under* Bangladesh

Easter (holiday)
DISCUSSIONS
Christianity *volume* **5** *page* **57**

Easter Island (island in the Pacific Ocean)
ARTICLE *volume* **9** *page* **89**

DISCUSSIONS
sculpture *volume* **3** *page* **11**
LEARN MORE *look under* islands; Pacific Ocean

Eastern Africa: *look under*
places: Ethiopia; Kenya; Kilimanjaro; Seychelles; Somalia; Uganda

Eastern Europe
DISCUSSIONS
folk arts and crafts photograph *volume* **3** *page* **6**
LEARN MORE *look under*
countries: Russia; Serbia and Montenegro; Ukraine
cities: Bucharest; Budapest; Istanbul; Sofia
other places: Danube

Eastern Orthodoxy (religion)
DISCUSSIONS
Christianity *volume* **5** *page* **57**

echidnas (animals): *look under* spiny anteaters

echoes
ARTICLE *volume* **1** *page* **68**
DISCUSSIONS
bats *volume* **12** *page* **89**
LEARN MORE *look under* waves

ecology: *look under* ecosystems

ecosystems
DISCUSSIONS
mongooses *volume* **12** *page* **36**
LEARN MORE *look under*
places: Amazon
types: deserts; marshes; oasis; rainforests; swamps

Edinburgh, *also called* Dun Eideann (city in Scotland, U.K.)
ARTICLE *volume* **6** *page* **23**
DISCUSSIONS
atlas *volume* **13** *page* **6**
LEARN MORE *look under* Scotland

Edinburgh Castle (castle in Edinburgh, Scotland, U.K.)
DISCUSSIONS
Edinburgh *volume* **6** *page* **23**, photograph *volume* **6** *page* **22**
LEARN MORE *look under* castles; Scotland

Edison, Thomas (American inventor)
DISCUSSIONS
Did you know? *volume* **2** *page* **57**

editing (motion pictures)
DISCUSSIONS
motion pictures *volume* **2** *page* **82**

education
DISCUSSIONS
Charlemagne *volume* **4** *page* **41**
Confucius *volume* **5** *page* **72**
Muslim schools photograph *volume* **5** *page* **69**
Socrates *volume* **4** *page* **24**

eggs
DISCUSSIONS
Did you know? *volume* **11** *page* **33**
folk arts and crafts photograph *volume* **3** *page* **6**
ostriches photograph *volume* **11** *page* **31**
platypuses *volume* **12** *page* **84**

Egypt (country)
ARTICLE *volume* **8** *page* **51**
DISCUSSIONS
atlas *volume* **13** *page* **12**
cats *volume* **12** *page* **21**
Did you know? *volume* **5** *page* **44**
flag *volume* **8** *page* **51**
Moses *volume* **5** *page* **54**
Nile River *volume* **8** *page* **54**
oasis *volume* **1** *page* **34**
peninsulas *volume* **1** *page* **22**
Pharaohs and the Pyramids *volume* **8** *page* **49**
Sadat Resthouse photograph *volume* **3** *page* **14**
LEARN MORE *look under*
people: Cleopatra; Fathy, Hassan; Sadat, Anwar el-
places: Cairo; North Africa
things: Anubis

Eiffel Tower (tower in Paris, France)
DISCUSSIONS
Did you know? *volume* **3** *page* **12**
Paris *volume* **6** *page* **35**, photograph *volume* **6** *page* **35**
LEARN MORE *look under* towers

Eightfold Path (religion)
DISCUSSIONS
Buddhism *volume* **5** *page* **81**

Einstein, Albert (German-American scientist)
ARTICLE *volume* **4** *page* **74**
LEARN MORE *look under* science

Eisteddfod (Welsh festival)
DISCUSSIONS
Wales *volume* **6** *page* **28**
LEARN MORE *look under* folk music

El Salvador (country)
DISCUSSIONS
Central America *volume* **9** *page* **45**

mangoes; nuts; olive; oranges; palms; peanuts; peppers; potatoes; strawberries; tea; tomatoes; yams
people: Burbank, Luther

Fuji, Mount (mountain in Japan)
DISCUSSIONS
atlas *volume* **13** *page* **8**
Japan *volume* **7** *page* **15,** photograph *volume* **7** *page* **15**
LEARN MORE *look under* mountains; volcanoes

Fulani (people)
DISCUSSIONS
Guinea *volume* **8** *page* **14**
LEARN MORE *look under* peoples; West Africa

Fundy, Bay of (bay in Canada)
DISCUSSIONS
tides *volume* **1** *page* **46**
LEARN MORE *look under* Canada

fungi
DISCUSSIONS
ants *volume* **11** *page* **59**

fuses
DISCUSSIONS
electricity *volume* **2** *page* **56**

Fushimi Inari shrine (building in Japan)
DISCUSSIONS
Shinto photograph *volume* **5** *page* **76**

Gaborone (city in Botswana)
DISCUSSIONS
Botswana *volume* **8** *page* **71**
LEARN MORE *look under* Botswana

Gaelic (language)
DISCUSSIONS
Did you know? *volume* **6** *page* **26**
LEARN MORE *look under* language

Gagarin, Yuri (Russian cosmonaut)
DISCUSSIONS
astronauts *volume* **2** *page* **19**

Galapagos Islands (islands in the Pacific Ocean)
ARTICLE *volume* **9** *page* **68**
LEARN MORE *look under* islands; Pacific Ocean; South America

galaxies
ARTICLE *volume* **2** *page* **13**
DISCUSSIONS
universe *volume* **2** *page* **9**
LEARN MORE *look under* solar system; stars

Galilee, Sea of (lake in Israel): *look under* Tiberias, Lake

Galileo Galilei (Italian astronomer, mathematician, and philosopher)
ARTICLE *volume* **4** *page* **77**
DISCUSSIONS
Saturn *volume* **2** *page* **39**
LEARN MORE *look under* astronomy; science
other astronomers: Copernicus, Nicolaus; Kepler, Johannes; Piazzi, Giuseppe

Gama, Vasco da (Portuguese explorer)
DISCUSSIONS
Portugal *volume* **6** *page* **8**
LEARN MORE *look under* exploration

Gandhi, Indira (Indian leader)
DISCUSSIONS
Did you know? *volume* **4** *page* **57**

Gandhi, Mahatma, *also called* Mohandas K. Gandhi (Indian leader)
ARTICLE *volume* **4** *page* **95**
DISCUSSIONS
Did you know? *volume* **8** *page* **84**
LEARN MORE *look under* India
other civil rights leaders: King, Martin Luther, Jr; Mandela, Nelson

Ganesha (Hindu god)
DISCUSSIONS
God *volume* **5** *page* **44**
Hinduism *volume* **5** *page* **79**

Ganges River, *also called* Ganga (river in Asia)
DISCUSSIONS
Did you know? *volume* **5** *page* **78,** photograph *volume* **5** *page* **79**
swamps *volume* **1** *page* **28**
LEARN MORE *look under* rivers
places: Bangladesh; India

Garay, Juan de (Spanish explorer)
DISCUSSIONS
Buenos Aires *volume* **9** *page* **93**
LEARN MORE *look under* exploration; Spain

gas (cooking and heating)
DISCUSSIONS
Did you know? *volume* **2** *page* **53**

gases (state of matter): *look under* liquids, solids, and gases

'Gates of Hell, The' (sculpture by Rodin)
DISCUSSIONS
Did you know? *volume* **3** *page* **24**

Gateway Arch (monument in United States)
DISCUSSIONS
United States photograph *volume* **9** *page* **27**
LEARN MORE *look under* architecture

gauchos (Argentinian cowboys)
DISCUSSIONS
Argentina *volume* **9** *page* **90**

Gautama (founder of Buddhism): *look under* Buddha

gazelles (animals)
ARTICLE *volume* **12** *page* **55**
LEARN MORE *look under* ungulates
similar animals: sheep; wild goats

Gdansk (city in Poland)
DISCUSSIONS
Poland photograph *volume* **6** *page* **56**

geckos (reptiles)
DISCUSSIONS
lizards photograph *volume* **11** *page* **85**

geese, *also called* goose
ARTICLE *volume* **11** *page* **22**
LEARN MORE *look under* birds

gemstones (minerals used as jewels)
DISCUSSIONS
volcanoes *volume* **1** *page* **15**
LEARN MORE *look under* diamonds

geochemistry (science)
DISCUSSIONS
geology *volume* **1** *page* **75**

geography (science)
ARTICLE *volume* **1** *page* **6**
LEARN MORE *look under* caves; continents; deserts; islands; marshes; mountains; oasis; oceans; peninsulas; rainforests; rivers; swamps; volcanoes

geology (science)
ARTICLE *volume* **1** *page* **75**
DISCUSSIONS
Marie Curie *volume* **4** *page* **71**
LEARN MORE *look under* caves; chalk; diamonds; fossils; oil; rocks and minerals; sand; thermal power; volcanoes

George, Saint (patron saint of England)
DISCUSSIONS
dragons *volume* **5** *page* **9**

Good Friday
DISCUSSIONS
Christianity *volume* **5** *page* **57**

Good Hope, Cape of (promontory in South Africa)
DISCUSSIONS
atlas photograph *volume* **13** *page* **13**
LEARN MORE *look under* Southern Africa

Good Queen Bess (queen of England): *look under* Elizabeth I

Goodall, Jane (British scientist)
ARTICLE *volume* **4** *page* **78**
LEARN MORE *look under* apes; science

goose: *look under* geese

gorals (mammals)
DISCUSSIONS
wild goats *volume* **12** *page* **58**

Gorée (island in Senegal)
DISCUSSIONS
Dakar *volume* **8** *page* **25**, photograph *volume* **8** *page* **24**
Senegal *volume* **8** *page* **23**

Gorgon (Greek myth)
DISCUSSIONS
Did you know? *volume* **5** *page* **29**

gorillas
ARTICLE *volume* **12** *page* **11**
DISCUSSIONS
apes *volume* **12** *page* **9**
LEARN MORE *look under* primates

Gospels (sacred text)
DISCUSSIONS
Bible *volume* **5** *page* **63**
Jesus Christ *volume* **5** *page* **58**

Gothic architecture
DISCUSSIONS
Notre-Dame de Paris photograph *volume* **3** *page* **13**

Gotthard Tunnel (tunnel in Switzerland)
DISCUSSIONS
Did you know? *volume* **6** *page* **47**

Goya, Francisco de (Spanish painter)
ARTICLE *volume* **4** *page* **14**
LEARN MORE *look under* painting

grafting (horticulture)
DISCUSSIONS
Luther Burbank *volume* **4** *page* **66**

Gran Colombia (historic republic in South America)

DISCUSSIONS
Bogotá *volume* **9** *page* **73**

Grand Canyon (canyon in Arizona, U.S.)
ARTICLE *volume* **9** *page* **32**
DISCUSSIONS
atlas *volume* **13** *page* **14**
LEARN MORE *look under* United States of America

'Granth Sahib' (holy book): *look under* 'Adi Granth'

Grant's gazelles
DISCUSSIONS
gazelles photograph *volume* **12** *page* **54**

grapes (fruit)
ARTICLE *volume* **10** *page* **25**
DISCUSSIONS
France *volume* **6** *page* **32**, photograph *volume* **6** *page* **33**
Switzerland *volume* **6** *page* **46**
LEARN MORE *look under* fruits and vegetables

grasses
ARTICLE *volume* **10** *page* **63**
DISCUSSIONS
rice *volume* **10** *page* **73**
LEARN MORE *look under* bamboo; barley; maize; marshes; plants; rice; rushes and reeds; sugarcane; wheat

grasshoppers (insects)
ARTICLE *volume* **11** *page* **69**
DISCUSSIONS
insects *volume* **11** *page* **57**
LEARN MORE *look under* crickets; insects

gravity
ARTICLE *volume* **2** *page* **50**
DISCUSSIONS
Albert Einstein *volume* **4** *page* **74**
Did you know? *volume* **2** *page* **16**
Moon *volume* **2** *page* **27**
oceans *volume* **1** *page* **37**
sand dunes photograph *volume* **1** *page* **18**
Sir Isaac Newton *volume* **4** *page* **83**
solar system *volume* **2** *page* **21**
tides *volume* **1** *page* **46**
LEARN MORE *look under* physical sciences

great apes
DISCUSSIONS
apes *volume* **12** *page* **9**
LEARN MORE *look under* gorillas

Great Barrier Reef (reef in Australia)
ARTICLE *volume* **7** *page* **92**
DISCUSSIONS
atlas *volume* **13** *page* **10**
Australia *volume* **7** *page* **89**
coral *volume* **11** *page* **45**, photograph *volume* **11** *page* **44**
LEARN MORE *look under* Australia; islands

Great Britain (country): *look under* United Kingdom

Great Dismal Swamp (swamp in the U.S.)
DISCUSSIONS
swamps *volume* **1** *page* **28**

Great Fire of London (English history)
DISCUSSIONS
Did you know? *volume* **6** *page* **16**

Great Lakes (lake system in North America)
ARTICLE *volume* **9** *page* **23**
DISCUSSIONS
atlas *volume* **13** *page* **14**
glaciers *volume* **1** *page* **54**
United States of America *volume* **9** *page* **25**
LEARN MORE *look under* lakes; North America

Great Pyramid (pyramid in Egypt)
DISCUSSIONS
Egypt *volume* **8** *page* **49**

Great Red Spot (feature of Jupiter)
DISCUSSIONS
Jupiter *volume* **2** *page* **36**, photograph *volume* **2** *page* **36**

Great Rift Valley (valley in Africa and Asia)
DISCUSSIONS
Kenya *volume* **8** *page* **30**

Great Star of Africa (gem diamond)
DISCUSSIONS
Did you know? *volume* **8** *page* **83**

'Great Train Robbery, The' (film by Porter)
DISCUSSIONS
cinema *volume* **3** *page* **75**, photograph *volume* **3** *page* **75**

Great Wall (wall in China)
ARTICLE *volume* **7** *page* **13**
DISCUSSIONS
atlas *volume* **13** *page* **8**
LEARN MORE *look under* architecture; China

jackals (animals)
DISCUSSIONS
Did you know? *volume* **12** *page* **29**

jackfruit
ARTICLE *volume* **10** *page* **55**
LEARN MORE *look under* fruits and vegetables; trees

jackrabbits
DISCUSSIONS
rabbits and hares photograph *volume* **12** *page* **92**

Jacob sheep
DISCUSSIONS
Did you know? *volume* **12** *page* **56**

Jaguar, Temple of the (temple in Guatemala): *look under* Giant Jaguar, Temple of the

Jainism (religion)
ARTICLE *volume* **5** *page* **87**
LEARN MORE *look under* Buddhism; Hinduism; monasticism; Sikhism

Jakarta (city in Indonesia)
DISCUSSIONS
atlas *volume* **13** *page* **8**
Indonesia *volume* **7** *page* **29**

Jamestown (city in Virginia, U.S.)
DISCUSSIONS
United States of America *volume* **9** *page* **27**

Japan (country)
ARTICLE *volume* **7** *page* **15**
DISCUSSIONS
atlas *volume* **13** *page* **8**
atomic bombs *volume* **2** *page* **62**
culture *volume* **7** *page* **16**
Did you know? *volume* **4** *page* **55**
flag *volume* **7** *page* **15**
macaques photograph *volume* **12** *page* **16**
Pyongyang *volume* **7** *page* **20**
Seoul *volume* **7** *page* **23**
Shinto *volume* **5** *page* **77**
theatre photograph *volume* **3** *page* **72**
LEARN MORE *look under*
people: Basho; Hirohito; Hiroshige; Kurosawa, Akira
religion: Buddhism; Daoism
things: earthquakes; tea; volcanoes

Japanese macaques (animals)
DISCUSSIONS
macaques *volume* **12** *page* **17**, photograph *volume* **12** *page* **16**

Java (island in Indonesia): *look under* Indonesia

jazz (music)
ARTICLE *volume* **3** *page* **35**
LEARN MORE *look under*
people: Armstrong, Louis; Basie, Count
things: popular music

Jean Bernard (cave in France)
DISCUSSIONS
caves *volume* **1** *page* **79**

Jefferson Memorial (monument in Washington, D.C., U.S.)
DISCUSSIONS
Washington, D.C. photograph *volume* **9** *page* **31**
LEARN MORE *look under* architecture

jellyfish (ocean animals)
ARTICLE *volume* **11** *page* **53**
LEARN MORE *look under* coral; marine animals

Jerusalem (city in Israel)
ARTICLE *volume* **7** *page* **77**
DISCUSSIONS
atlas *volume* **13** *page* **8**
Islam photograph *volume* **5** *page* **64**
Israel *volume* **7** *page* **75**
Judaism photograph *volume* **5** *page* **51**
Menachem Begin photograph *volume* **4** *page* **34**
Muhammad *volume* **5** *page* **67**
LEARN MORE *look under* Middle East

Jesus Christ
ARTICLE *volume* **5** *page* **58**
LEARN MORE *look under* Bible
other biblical people: Abraham; Mary; Moses
religions: Christianity; Islam; Roman Catholicism
other religious leaders: Buddha; Confucius; Muhammad; Zoroaster

jewellery
DISCUSSIONS
Did you know? *volume* **8** *page* **90**
diamonds *volume* **1** *page* **80**, photograph *volume* **1** *page* **80**

jihads (religion): *look under* holy wars

Jina (religion)
DISCUSSIONS
Jainism *volume* **5** *page* **87**

jingxi (music): *look under* Peking opera

Jinnah, Mohammed Ali (Pakistani leader)
ARTICLE *volume* **4** *page* **51**
LEARN MORE *look under* Pakistan
other independence leaders: Gandhi, Mahatma; Mandela, Nelson

joeys (kangaroos)
ARTICLE *volume* **12** *page* **78**

Johannesburg (city in South Africa)
DISCUSSIONS
atlas *volume* **13** *page* **12**
Did you know? *volume* **8** *page* **86**
South Africa *volume* **8** *page* **82**

Johnny Clegg and Savuka (South African musical group)
DISCUSSIONS
popular music photograph *volume* **3** *page* **33**
LEARN MORE *look under* Ladysmith Black Mambazo

Jordan (country)
DISCUSSIONS
atlas *volume* **13** *page* **8**
flag *volume* **7** *page* **79**
LEARN MORE *look under* Amman; Middle East

'Journey to the Centre of the Earth, A' (book by Verne)
DISCUSSIONS
Jules Verne *volume* **3** *page* **68**

Judaism (religion)
ARTICLE *volume* **5** *page* **50**
DISCUSSIONS
calendars illustration *volume* **2** *page* **77**
God *volume* **5** *page* **44**
Israel *volume* **7** *page* **75**
Sinai Peninsula *volume* **1** *page* **22**
LEARN MORE *look under*
people: Abraham; Frank, Anne; Moses
stories: 'Golem of Prague, The'
writings: Bible
similar religions: Christianity; Islam

'Julius Caesar' (play by Shakespeare)
DISCUSSIONS
Did you know? *volume* **4** *page* **36**

jumping spiders
DISCUSSIONS
spiders *volume* **11** *page* **72**, photograph *volume* **11** *page* **72**

Jupiter (planet)
ARTICLE *volume* **2** *page* **36**

language: *look under* click languages; English language; Gaelic; Quechua; sign language

Laozi (Chinese philosopher)
DISCUSSIONS
Daoism *volume* **5** *page* **74**

laptop computers, *also called* notebook computers
DISCUSSIONS
computers *volume* **2** *page* **79**

latex (chemical)
DISCUSSIONS
rubber trees *volume* **10** *page* **90,**
photograph *volume* **10** *page* **90**

Latin America: *look under*
people: Allende, Isabel; Bolívar, Simón
places: Central America; South America

lava (volcanoes)
DISCUSSIONS
mountains *volume* **1** *page* **16**
volcanoes *volume* **1** *page* **15**

Law (Jewish writings): *look under* Torah

layering (farming)
DISCUSSIONS
grapes *volume* **10** *page* **25**

leaders: *look under* Arafat, Yasir; Ashoka; Begin, Menachem; Bolívar, Simón; Caesar, Julius; Castro, Fidel; Charlemagne; Cleopatra; Elizabeth I; Empress of China; Hirohito; Jinnah, Mohammed Ali; Mandela, Nelson; Mao Zedong; Meir, Golda; Sadat, Anwar el-; Thant, U

leaf-nosed bats (animals)
DISCUSSIONS
bats photograph *volume* **12** *page* **89**

Leakey, Louis (Kenyan scientist)
DISCUSSIONS
Jane Goodall *volume* **4** *page* **78**
LEARN MORE *look under* science

Leaning Tower of Pisa (tower in Pisa, Italy)
DISCUSSIONS
Europe photograph *volume* **6** *page* **6**
Italy *volume* **6** *page* **89**
LEARN MORE *look under* towers

leather carp (fish)
DISCUSSIONS
carp *volume* **11** *page* **37**
LEARN MORE *look under* fish

leatherback turtles (turtles)
DISCUSSIONS
reptiles *volume* **11** *page* **75**

leaves
ARTICLE *volume* **1** *page* **67**
LEARN MORE *look under* cabbage; plants; tea

Lebanon (country)
DISCUSSIONS
atlas *volume* **13** *page* **8**
flag *volume* **7** *page* **79**
Menachem Begin *volume* **4** *page* **35**
LEARN MORE *look under* Beirut; Fertile Crescent; Middle East

legends
ARTICLE *volume* **5** *page* **7**
LEARN MORE *look under*
stories: Bunyan, Paul; dragons; 'Golem of Prague, The'; Knights of the Round Table; 'Odysseus and the Cyclops'; Trojan Horse, The
other things: Abominable Snowman; Atlantis; fables; folktales; mermaids; myths

legumes (plants)
DISCUSSIONS
peanuts *volume* **10** *page* **30**
LEARN MORE *look under* plants

lemons
ARTICLE *volume* **10** *page* **47**
LEARN MORE *look under* fruits and vegetables; trees

lemurs (animals)
ARTICLE *volume* **12** *page* **19**
LEARN MORE *look under* primates

L'Enfant, Pierre-Charles (French engineer and artist)
DISCUSSIONS
Washington, D.C., U.S. *volume* **9** *page* **31**

lens
DISCUSSIONS
photography *volume* **2** *page* **88**
telescopes *volume* **2** *page* **103**

leprechauns (Irish folklore)
DISCUSSIONS
Did you know? *volume* **6** *page* **25**

leprosy (disease)
DISCUSSIONS
Did you know? *volume* **12** *page* **86**

Leshan Buddha (statue)
DISCUSSIONS
Did you know? *volume* **5** *page* **80**

lesser apes
DISCUSSIONS
apes *volume* **12** *page* **9**
LEARN MORE *look under* gibbons

lesser pandas, *also called* cat bears, *or* red bear cats (animals)
DISCUSSIONS
pandas *volume* **12** *page* **38,**
photograph *volume* **12** *page* **38**

Liberia (country)
ARTICLE *volume* **8** *page* **17**
DISCUSSIONS
atlas *volume* **13** *page* **12**
flag *volume* **8** *page* **17**
LEARN MORE *look under*
places: Monrovia; West Africa

Library of Congress (library in Washington, D.C., U.S.)
DISCUSSIONS
Did you know? *volume* **9** *page* **31**

Libya (country)
ARTICLE *volume* **8** *page* **58**
DISCUSSIONS
atlas *volume* **13** *page* **12**
Did you know? *volume* **1** *page* **34**
flag *volume* **8** *page* **58**
LEARN MORE *look under*
places: North Africa; Tripoli

life
DISCUSSIONS
Buddhism *volume* **5** *page* **81**
Confucius *volume* **5** *page* **72**
energy *volume* **2** *page* **48**
extraterrestrial life *volume* **2** *page* **14**
God *volume* **5** *page* **44**
LEARN MORE *look under* animals; bacteria; fossils; plants

'Life on the Mississippi' (book by Twain)
DISCUSSIONS
Mark Twain *volume* **4** *page* **29**

Liffey, River (river in Ireland)
DISCUSSIONS
Dublin *volume* **6** *page* **26,** photograph *volume* **6** *page* **27**
LEARN MORE *look under* rivers

light
DISCUSSIONS
Albert Einstein *volume* **4** *page* **74**
energy *volume* **2** *page* **48**
rainbows *volume* **1** *page* **63**
LEARN MORE *look under* bioluminescence; colour

light bulbs: *look under* electricity

lightning (weather): *look under* thunder and lightning

Lilongwe (city in Malawi)
ARTICLE *volume* **8** *page* **77**
DISCUSSIONS
atlas *volume* **13** *page* **12**
Malawi *volume* **8** *page* **75**
LEARN MORE *look under* Malawi

Lima (city in Peru): *look under* Peru

limestone (rock)
DISCUSSIONS
chalk *volume* **1** *page* **83**
rocks and minerals *volume* **1** *page* **76**

Lincoln, Abraham (American leader)
DISCUSSIONS
Did you know? *volume* **3** *page* **50**

Lincoln Memorial (monument in Washington, D.C., U.S.)
DISCUSSIONS
Washington, D.C. photograph *volume* **9** *page* **30**

lion-tailed macaques (animals)
DISCUSSIONS
macaques *volume* **12** *page* **17**

lions
ARTICLE *volume* **12** *page* **24**
LEARN MORE *look under* carnivores; cats; ocelots; tigers

lip-reading
DISCUSSIONS
deafness *volume* **2** *page* **96**

liquids, solids, and gases (states of matter)
ARTICLE *volume* **2** *page* **52**
LEARN MORE *look under* atoms; physical sciences

Lisbon (city in Portugal)
DISCUSSIONS
atlas *volume* **13** *page* **6**
Portugal *volume* **6** *page* **8**
LEARN MORE *look under* Portugal

literature (art)
ARTICLE *volume* **3** *page* **50**
LEARN MORE *look under* Bible; fables; folktales; Koran; writing
people: Allende, Isabel; Basho; Borges, Jorge Luis; Brooks, Gwendolyn; Carroll, Lewis; Dickens, Charles; Dickinson, Emily; Frank, Anne; Keller, Helen; Shakespeare, William; Soyinka, Wole; Tagore, Rabindranath; Twain, Mark; Verne, Jules; Walker, Kath
places: England

Literature, Temple of (temple in Hanoi, Vietnam)
DISCUSSIONS
Hanoi *volume* **7** *page* **42**
LEARN MORE *look under* temples

Little Mermaid (statue)
DISCUSSIONS
Copenhagen *volume* **6** *page* **62**
LEARN MORE *look under* fairy tales

lizards
ARTICLE *volume* **11** *page* **85**
DISCUSSIONS
reptiles *volume* **11** *page* **75**
LEARN MORE *look under* alligators and crocodiles; chameleons; dinosaurs; Komodo dragons; reptiles

llamas (animals)
ARTICLE *volume* **12** *page* **62**
DISCUSSIONS
Chile photograph *volume* **9** *page* **87**
Did you know? *volume* **9** *page* **75**
LEARN MORE *look under* camels; ungulates

Llanos (region in South America)
DISCUSSIONS
Colombia *volume* **9** *page* **71**
LEARN MORE *look under* South America

loa (voodoo)
DISCUSSIONS
Vodun *volume* **5** *page* **92**

Loch Ness (lake in Scotland)
DISCUSSIONS
Scotland *volume* **6** *page* **21**
LEARN MORE *look under* lakes; myths

locks (canals)
DISCUSSIONS
Panama Canal *volume* **9** *page* **52**
LEARN MORE *look under* ships

locusts (insects)
DISCUSSIONS
insects *volume* **11** *page* **57**

London (city in England, U.K.)
ARTICLE *volume* **6** *page* **16**
DISCUSSIONS
atlas *volume* **13** *page* **6**
England photograph *volume* **6** *page* **15**
LEARN MORE *look under* England

long (Chinese mythology): *look under* dragons

longhorn cattle (animals)
DISCUSSIONS
cattle photograph *volume* **12** *page* **46**

longships, *also called* dragon ships
DISCUSSIONS
Vikings *volume* **4** *page* **62**, photograph *volume* **4** *page* **63**

loom (weaving machine)
DISCUSSIONS
Did you know? *volume* **2** *page* **79**
weaving *volume* **2** *page* **108**, photograph *volume* **2** *page* **109**

Lotus Temple (temple in India)
DISCUSSIONS
architecture photograph *volume* **3** *page* **12**
LEARN MORE *look under* temples

Louvre (museum in Paris, France)
DISCUSSIONS
I. M. Pei *volume* **4** *page* **18**, photograph *volume* **4** *page* **18**, photograph *volume* **4** *page* **19**
LEARN MORE *look under* Paris
things: painting; sculpture

Luanda (city in Angola)
ARTICLE *volume* **8** *page* **68**
DISCUSSIONS
atlas *volume* **13** *page* **12**
LEARN MORE *look under* Angola

Luc Thuy (lake in Hanoi, Vietnam): *look under* Hoan Kiem, Lake

Lucas, George (American film director and producer)
DISCUSSIONS
Akira Kurosawa photograph *volume* **3** *page* **86**

'Lucia di Lammermoor' (opera by Donizetti)
DISCUSSIONS
Joan Sutherland *volume* **4** *page* **27**

Lucy (human ancestor)
DISCUSSIONS
Did you know? *volume* **8** *page* **26**
LEARN MORE *look under* human beings

lumberjacks
DISCUSSIONS
Paul Bunyan *volume* **5** *page* **39**

lungfish
DISCUSSIONS
Did you know? *volume* **11** *page* **34**
LEARN MORE *look under* marine animals

Lyme Regis (city in England, U.K.)
DISCUSSIONS
English Channel photograph *volume* **6** *page* **31**

Ma-Xia school (painting)
DISCUSSIONS
Xia Gui *volume* **3** *page* **28**

Mabovitch, Goldie (Israeli leader): *look under* Meir, Golda

macaques (animals)
ARTICLE *volume* **12** *page* **17**
LEARN MORE *look under* monkeys

macaws (birds)
DISCUSSIONS
parrots and cockatoos *volume* **11** *page* **11**, photograph *volume* **11** *page* **11**

Machu Picchu (ancient Inca city in Peru)
ARTICLE *volume* **9** *page* **77**
DISCUSSIONS
llamas photograph *volume* **12** *page* **63**
LEARN MORE *look under* American Indians; Andes

Mackenzie River (river in Canada)
DISCUSSIONS
Aklavik photograph *volume* **9** *page* **12**
LEARN MORE *look under* rivers

Madagascar (country)
ARTICLE *volume* **8** *page* **73**
DISCUSSIONS
atlas *volume* **13** *page* **12**
LEARN MORE *look under* islands; Southern Africa
animals: chameleons; lemurs

Madonna, the (mother of Jesus): *look under* Mary

'Madonna della Pietà' (sculpture by Michelangelo)
DISCUSSIONS
Michelangelo *volume* **3** *page* **21**

'Madonna of Humility' (painting by Angelico)
DISCUSSIONS
Mary illustration *volume* **5** *page* **60**

madrasahs (Muslim schools)
DISCUSSIONS
Pakistani students photograph *volume* **5** *page* **69**

Madrid (city in Spain)
ARTICLE *volume* **6** *page* **13**
DISCUSSIONS
atlas *volume* **13** *page* **6**
LEARN MORE *look under* Spain

Magdalen Islands (islands in Canada)
DISCUSSIONS
Did you know? *volume* **9** *page* **16**

Magellan (U.S. space probe)
DISCUSSIONS
Did you know? *volume* **4** *page* **100**
launch from space shuttle photograph *volume* **2** *page* **33**
LEARN MORE *look under* exploration; spacecraft

Magellan, Ferdinand (Portuguese explorer)
ARTICLE *volume* **4** *page* **101**
DISCUSSIONS
Portugal *volume* **6** *page* **8**
LEARN MORE *look under* exploration

Magellan, Strait of (channel in South America)
DISCUSSIONS
atlas *volume* **13** *page* **17**
Ferdinand Magellan *volume* **4** *page* **101**

'Magic Flute, The' (opera by Mozart)
DISCUSSIONS
opera *volume* **3** *page* **76**

magic realism (literature)
DISCUSSIONS
Isabel Allende *volume* **4** *page* **7**

magma (molten rock)
DISCUSSIONS
rocks and minerals *volume* **1** *page* **76**
volcanoes *volume* **1** *page* **15**

magnets
DISCUSSIONS
electricity *volume* **2** *page* **56**

Mahavira (founder of Jainism)
DISCUSSIONS
Jainism *volume* **5** *page* **87**, photograph *volume* **5** *page* **86**

Mahé (island in Seychelles)
DISCUSSIONS
Seychelles *volume* **8** *page* **35**

'Maids of Honour, The' (painting by Velázquez): *look under* 'Meninas, Las'

main memory (computer science)
DISCUSSIONS
computers *volume* **2** *page* **79**

maize (plants)
ARTICLE *volume* **10** *page* **70**
LEARN MORE *look under* fruits and vegetables; grasses

malachite kingfishers (birds)
DISCUSSIONS
kingfishers photograph *volume* **11** *page* **9**

Malagasy (people)
DISCUSSIONS
Madagascar *volume* **8** *page* **73**
LEARN MORE *look under* peoples

malaria (disease)
DISCUSSIONS
Did you know? *volume* **11** *page* **71**

Malawi (country)
ARTICLE *volume* **8** *page* **75**
DISCUSSIONS
atlas *volume* **13** *page* **12**
flag *volume* **8** *page* **75**
LEARN MORE *look under* Lilongwe; Southern Africa

Malawi, Lake (lake in Africa)
DISCUSSIONS
Malawi *volume* **8** *page* **75**, photograph *volume* **8** *page* **74**
LEARN MORE *look under* Africa; lakes

Malayan lars (apes): *look under* white-handed gibbons

Malaysia (country)
DISCUSSIONS
atlas *volume* **13** *page* **8**
tea photograph *volume* **10** *page* **38**
LEARN MORE *look under*
animals: tapirs
places: Southeast Asia

Maldives (island country)
DISCUSSIONS
atlas *volume* **13** *page* **8**
island photograph *volume* **1** *page* **13**

Malinke (people)
DISCUSSIONS
Guinea *volume* **8** *page* **14**

mambos (Vodun priestesses)
DISCUSSIONS
Vodun *volume* **5** *page* **92**

mammals (animals)
VOLUME **12**
LEARN MORE *look under* animals; armadillos; bats; carnivores; manatees; marsupials; platypuses; primates; rabbits and hares; rodents; ungulates; whales

Mammoth Cave-Flint Ridge (cave system in the U.S.)
DISCUSSIONS
caves *volume* **1** *page* **79**

Mazar-e Sharif (city in Afghanistan)
DISCUSSIONS
Afghanistan photograph *volume* **7** *page* **44**

Mbundu (people)
DISCUSSIONS
Angola *volume* **8** *page* **67**
LEARN MORE *look under* peoples

McKinley, Mount, *also called* Denali (mountain in Alaska, U.S.)
DISCUSSIONS
atlas photograph *volume* **13** *page* **15**
United States of America *volume* **9** *page* **25**
LEARN MORE *look under* Alaska; mountains

measurement
ARTICLE *volume* **2** *page* **59**
LEARN MORE *look under* calendars

Mecca (city in Saudi Arabia)
ARTICLE *volume* **7** *page* **84**
DISCUSSIONS
atlas *volume* **13** *page* **8**
Islam *volume* **5** *page* **64**
Kaaba photograph *volume* **5** *page* **66**
Muhammad *volume* **5** *page* **67**
LEARN MORE *look under* Islam; Saudi Arabia

medicine (science)
ARTICLE *volume* **2** *page* **60**
DISCUSSIONS
Did you know? *volume* **6** *page* **82**, *volume* **9** *page* **64**
macaques *volume* **12** *page* **17**
Marie Curie *volume* **4** *page* **71**
nuclear energy *volume* **2** *page* **62**
rainforests *volume* **1** *page* **24**
LEARN MORE *look under*
people: Blackwell, Elizabeth; Pasteur, Louis
things: Hippocratic oath

Medina (city in Saudi Arabia)
DISCUSSIONS
Did you know? *volume* **5** *page* **65**
Muhammad *volume* **5** *page* **67**

meditation
DISCUSSIONS
Baha'i *volume* **5** *page* **70**
Buddhism *volume* **5** *page* **81**
Hinduism *volume* **5** *page* **79**
monasticism *volume* **5** *page* **46**

Mediterranean Sea
ARTICLE *volume* **1** *page* **44**
DISCUSSIONS
atlas *volume* **13** *page* **6**, *volume* **13** *page* **8**, *volume* **13** *page* **12**

Suez Canal *volume* **8** *page* **56**
LEARN MORE *look under* Middle East; North Africa; Southern Europe

mediums (occultism)
DISCUSSIONS
Did you know? *volume* **6** *page* **59**

meerkats (animals): *look under* yellow mongooses

Meir, Golda, *also called* Goldie Mabovitch, *or* Goldie Myerson (Israeli leader)
ARTICLE *volume* **4** *page* **57**
LEARN MORE *look under* Israel
other Middle Eastern leaders: Arafat, Yasir; Begin, Menachem; Sadat, Anwar el-

'Meninas, Las', *also called* 'The Maids of Honour' (painting by Velázquez)
DISCUSSIONS
Madrid photograph *volume* **6** *page* **12**

menorahs (candelabra)
DISCUSSIONS
Judaism photograph *volume* **5** *page* **50**

Mercury (planet)
ARTICLE *volume* **2** *page* **30**
DISCUSSIONS
solar system illustration *volume* **2** *page* **20**
LEARN MORE *look under* planets

Merino sheep (animals)
DISCUSSIONS
New Zealand *volume* **7** *page* **99**
LEARN MORE *look under* sheep

Merlin (legendary magician)
DISCUSSIONS
Knights of the Round Table *volume* **5** *page* **33**

mermaids (legendary beings)
DISCUSSIONS
manatees *volume* **12** *page* **73**
LEARN MORE *look under* legends

Mesopotamia (ancient region in Asia)
DISCUSSIONS
transportation *volume* **2** *page* **106**

Messiah (religion)
DISCUSSIONS
Did you know? *volume* **5** *page* **58**

metals
DISCUSSIONS
electricity *volume* **2** *page* **56**

metamorphic rocks
DISCUSSIONS
rocks and minerals *volume* **1** *page* **76**

meteorites (astronomy)
DISCUSSIONS
tsunamis *volume* **1** *page* **50**

metric system (measurement system)
DISCUSSIONS
measurement *volume* **2** *page* **59**

Metropolitan Museum of Art (museum in New York City, U.S.)
DISCUSSIONS
New York City *volume* **9** *page* **38**, photograph *volume* **9** *page* **39**

Mexican bats (animals)
DISCUSSIONS
bats *volume* **12** *page* **89**

Mexico (country)
ARTICLE *volume* **9** *page* **41**
DISCUSSIONS
atlas *volume* **13** *page* **14**
Did you know? *volume* **3** *page* **7**
flag *volume* **9** *page* **41**
peninsulas *volume* **1** *page* **22**
LEARN MORE *look under*
people: Kahlo, Frida; Rivera, Diego; Santana, Carlos
places: Mexico City
things: Mayan Civilization

Mexico City, *also called* Tenochtitlán (city in Mexico)
ARTICLE *volume* **9** *page* **43**
DISCUSSIONS
atlas *volume* **13** *page* **14**
LEARN MORE *look under* Mexico

Michelangelo (Italian artist)
ARTICLE *volume* **3** *page* **21**
DISCUSSIONS
Moses photograph *volume* **5** *page* **55**
Vatican City *volume* **6** *page* **93**
LEARN MORE *look under* architecture; painting; sculpture
other famous Italians: Galileo Galilei; Marconi, Guglielmo; Piazzi, Giuseppe

Michigan (state in the U.S.)
DISCUSSIONS
peninsula photograph *volume* **1** *page* **22**

Michigan, Lake (lake in the U.S.)
DISCUSSIONS
Great Lakes *volume* **9** *page* **23**, photograph *volume* **9** *page* **22**, photograph *volume* **9** *page* **23**

Michinomiya Hirohito (emperor of Japan): *look under* Hirohito

microbiology: *look under* Pasteur, Louis

microprocessors (computer science)
DISCUSSIONS
computers *volume* **2** *page* **79**

Mid-Oceanic Ridge, *also called* Mid-Ocean Ridge
DISCUSSIONS
Did you know? *volume* **1** *page* **43**
oceans *volume* **1** *page* **37**

Middle East (region in Asia): *look under*
people: Arafat, Yasir; Begin, Menachem; Fathy, Hassan; Meir, Golda
places: Amman; Baghdad; Beirut; Damascus; Fertile Crescent; Iran; Israel; Istanbul; Jerusalem; Mecca; Mediterranean Sea; Mesopotamia; Oman; Palestine; Suez Canal
religions: Baha'i; Christianity; Islam; Judaism; Zoroastrianism
animals: camels; wild goats

'Midsummer Night's Dream, A' (play by Shakespeare)
DISCUSSIONS
William Shakespeare *volume* **4** *page* **23**, photograph *volume* **4** *page* **23**

mild peppers (plants): *look under* peppers

military
DISCUSSIONS
Braille *volume* **2** *page* **75**
Did you know? *volume* **11** *page* **87**

milk (food)
DISCUSSIONS
Louis Pasteur *volume* **4** *page* **85**
mammals *volume* **12** *page* **6**
LEARN MORE *look under* food

Milky Way Galaxy
DISCUSSIONS
galaxies *volume* **2** *page* **13**, photograph *volume* **2** *page* **12**

minerals: *look under* rocks and minerals

minor planets: *look under* asteroids

miracles
DISCUSSIONS
Jesus Christ *volume* **5** *page* **58**

mirror carp (fish)
DISCUSSIONS
carp *volume* **11** *page* **37**
LEARN MORE *look under* fish

mirrors
DISCUSSIONS
telescopes *volume* **2** *page* **103**

Mirza Ali Mohammad (Muslim leader): *look under* Bab, the

Mirza Hoseyn Ali Nuri (Iranian religious leader): *look under* Baha Ullah

Mississippi River (river in the United States)
DISCUSSIONS
atlas photograph *volume* **13** *page* **15**
Mark Twain *volume* **4** *page* **29**
United States of America *volume* **9** *page* **25**
LEARN MORE *look under* rivers

Mittens (rock formation in the United States)
DISCUSSIONS
United States photograph *volume* **9** *page* **25**

moai (statues)
DISCUSSIONS
Easter Island *volume* **9** *page* **89**, photograph *volume* **9** *page* **88**, photograph *volume* **9** *page* **89**
LEARN MORE *look under* arts

mobile phones, *also called* cell phones, *or* mobile cellular telephones
DISCUSSIONS
telephones *volume* **2** *page* **100**

mobiles (sculptures)
DISCUSSIONS
sculpture *volume* **3** *page* **11**

Model T (automobile)
DISCUSSIONS
automobiles *volume* **2** *page* **72**

modern dance
DISCUSSIONS
dance *volume* **3** *page* **70**

Mogadishu (city in Somalia)
ARTICLE *volume* **8** *page* **38**
DISCUSSIONS
atlas *volume* **13** *page* **12**
Somalia *volume* **8** *page* **36**
LEARN MORE *look under* Eastern Africa

Mohenjo-daro (ancient city in Pakistan)
DISCUSSIONS
ancient city site photograph *volume* **7** *page* **61**
Pakistan *volume* **7** *page* **60**
stone tablets photograph *volume* **7** *page* **60**

molasses (syrup)
DISCUSSIONS
sugarcane *volume* **10** *page* **76**
LEARN MORE *look under* sugarcane

molecules
DISCUSSIONS
atoms *volume* **2** *page* **46**

molluscs (animals)
ARTICLE *volume* **11** *page* **49**
LEARN MORE *look under* animals; aquatic animals; octopuses

monarch butterflies (insects)
DISCUSSIONS
Did you know? *volume* **11** *page* **63**

monasteries (religion): *look under* monasticism

monasticism (religion)
ARTICLE *volume* **5** *page* **46**
DISCUSSIONS
Buddhism photograph *volume* **5** *page* **81**
Jainism *volume* **5** *page* **87**
Shinto photograph *volume* **5** *page* **77**
Thailand photograph *volume* **7** *page* **36**
LEARN MORE *look under*
people: Buddha; Dalai Lama

mongooses (animals)
ARTICLE *volume* **12** *page* **36**
LEARN MORE *look under* carnivores; king cobras

Moni Mekhala and Ream Eyso (Cambodian myth)
ARTICLE *volume* **5** *page* **16**
LEARN MORE *look under*
other Asian stories: 'Poor Man and the Flask of Oil, The'; 'Tiger in the Trap, The'; 'Yeh-Shen'
other myths: Atlas; 'How Crow Brought Daylight to the World'

'Monkey Court, The' (Nigerian folktale)
ARTICLE *volume* **5** *page* **10**
LEARN MORE *look under*
other African stories: 'Ananse and the Wisdom Pot'
other folktales: 'How Kangaroo Got His Tail'; 'Poor Man and the Flask of Oil, The'; 'Rabbit Throws Away His Sandal'; 'Tiger in the Trap, The'; 'Why Possum's Tail Is Bare'; 'Yeh-Shen'

monkeys
ARTICLE *volume* **12** *page* **15**

mudskippers (fish): *look under* marine animals

Muhammad (prophet of Islam)
ARTICLE *volume* **5** *page* **67**
DISCUSSIONS
Islam *volume* **5** *page* **64**
LEARN MORE *look under* Islam; Koran
other people important to Islam:
Abraham; Jesus Christ; Moses
other founders of religions: Buddha;
Confucius; Zoroaster

mules (animals)
DISCUSSIONS
donkeys *volume* **12** *page* **42**

mummies
DISCUSSIONS
Did you know? *volume* **6** *page* **61**
Egypt *volume* **8** *page* **49**

Mumtaz Mahal, *also called* Arjumand Banu Baygam (Mughal queen)
DISCUSSIONS
Taj Mahal *volume* **7** *page* **52**

Muppets (puppets)
DISCUSSIONS
Jim Henson *volume* **3** *page* **85**, photograph *volume* **3** *page* **84**

murals (paintings)
DISCUSSIONS
Diego Rivera *volume* **3** *page* **22**, illustration *volume* **3** *page* **22**
painting *volume* **3** *page* **8**

music: *look under*
types of music: classical music; folk music; jazz; popular music
other things: musical instruments; opera; orchestra
non-Western music: Khan, Nusrat Fateh Ali; Ladysmith Black Mambazo; Shankar, Ravi
places: Vienna

musical instruments
DISCUSSIONS
jazz photograph *volume* **3** *page* **34**
Korean Peninsula *volume* **7** *page* **19**
Louis Armstrong photograph *volume* **3** *page* **38**
LEARN MORE *look under* guitars; piano; rhythm instruments; sitars

muskrats (animals)
ARTICLE *volume* **12** *page* **69**
LEARN MORE *look under* porcupines; rabbits and hares; raccoons
for other animals that live in water look under: aquatic animals

Muslims: *look under* Islam

mussels (animals)
DISCUSSIONS
molluscs photograph *volume* **11** *page* **48**

Myanmar (country)
DISCUSSIONS
atlas *volume* **13** *page* **8**
Buddhism photograph *volume* **5** *page* **81**
Yangôn *volume* **7** *page* **30**
LEARN MORE *look under*
people: Thant, U
animals: lesser pandas; tapirs

Myerson, Goldie (Israeli leader): *look under* Meir, Golda

mythology: *look under* myths

myths
ARTICLE *volume* **5** *page* **7**
DISCUSSIONS
Did you know? *volume* **5** *page* **77**
God *volume* **5** *page* **44**
LEARN MORE *look under*
stories: Atlas; 'How Crow Brought Daylight to the World'; Moni Mekhala and Ream Eyso
other things: fables; folktales; Greek mythology; legends

Nairobi (city in Kenya)
ARTICLE *volume* **8** *page* **33**
DISCUSSIONS
atlas *volume* **13** *page* **12**
LEARN MORE *look under* Eastern Africa; Kenya

Namib (desert in Africa)
DISCUSSIONS
Namibia *volume* **8** *page* **78**
LEARN MORE *look under* deserts

Namibia (country)
ARTICLE *volume* **8** *page* **78**
DISCUSSIONS
atlas *volume* **13** *page* **12**
flag *volume* **8** *page* **78**
LEARN MORE *look under* Southern Africa; Windhoek

Nanak, Guru (Indian religious leader)
DISCUSSIONS
Sikhism *volume* **5** *page* **88**

NASA, *also called* National Aeronautics and Space Administration (U.S. space agency)
DISCUSSIONS
Did you know? *volume* **2** *page* **58**
LEARN MORE *look under* astronauts; spacecraft

Nascimento, Edson Arantes do (Brazilian football player): *look under* Pelé

Nasser, Gamal Abdel (Egyptian leader)
DISCUSSIONS
Anwar el-Sadat *volume* **4** *page* **59**
LEARN MORE *look under* Egypt; Middle East

National Aeronautics and Space Administration (U.S. space agency): *look under* NASA

National Botanic Gardens (garden in Canberra, Australia)
DISCUSSIONS
Canberra *volume* **7** *page* **91**

nations: *look under* countries

Native Americans: *look under* American Indians

natural selection, *also called* survival of the fittest (biology)
DISCUSSIONS
Charles Darwin *volume* **4** *page* **73**
Galapagos Islands *volume* **9** *page* **68**

'Nautilus' (submarine)
DISCUSSIONS
Did you know? *volume* **2** *page* **99**

Navajo (people)
DISCUSSIONS
sand painting photograph *volume* **3** *page* **8**
LEARN MORE *look under* American Indians

navel oranges (fruit)
DISCUSSIONS
oranges photograph *volume* **10** *page* **48**

navjote (religion)
DISCUSSIONS
Zoroastrianism photograph *volume* **5** *page* **48**
LEARN MORE *look under* Bar Mitzvah

Nazis (German political movement)
DISCUSSIONS
Anne Frank *volume* **4** *page* **91**

Oahu (island in Hawaii, U.S.)
DISCUSSIONS
Honolulu *volume* **9** *page* **35**

oasis
ARTICLE *volume* **1** *page* **34**
DISCUSSIONS
deserts *volume* **1** *page* **20**
LEARN MORE *look under* geography; water

ocean liners (ships)
DISCUSSIONS
ships photograph *volume* **2** *page* **94**

ocean trenches
DISCUSSIONS
Pacific Ocean *volume* **1** *page* **41**
LEARN MORE *look under* Mariana Trench

oceans
ARTICLE *volume* **1** *page* **37**
DISCUSSIONS
deep-sea life *volume* **11** *page* **54**
pollution *volume* **1** *page* **73**
sand *volume* **1** *page* **18**
LEARN MORE *look under*
animals and plants: coral; deep-sea life; fish; gulls; jellyfish; manatees; molluscs; octopuses; penguins; salmon; seaweed; sharks; sponges; turtles; walruses; whales
oceans and seas: Atlantic Ocean; Indian Ocean; Mediterranean Sea; Pacific Ocean
other things: tides; water; waves

ocelots (animals)
ARTICLE *volume* **12** *page* **27**
LEARN MORE *look under* carnivores; cats; lions; tigers

octopuses (ocean animals)
ARTICLE *volume* **11** *page* **51**
LEARN MORE *look under* marine animals; molluscs

Odysseus (Greek legend)
DISCUSSIONS
Odysseus and the Cyclops *volume* **5** *page* **27**

'Odysseus and the Cyclops' (Greek legend)
ARTICLE *volume* **5** *page* **27**
LEARN MORE *look under*
other Greek stories: Aesop's fables; Atlas; Trojan Horse, The

other legends: Bunyan, Paul; dragons; 'Golem of Prague, The'; Knights of the Round Table

Ogun (Yoruba god)
DISCUSSIONS
Did you know? *volume* **3** *page* **63**

oil, *also called* petroleum
ARTICLE *volume* **2** *page* **84**
DISCUSSIONS
Oman *volume* **7** *page* **82**
LEARN MORE *look under* automobiles; pollution; 'Poor Man and the Flask of Oil, The'
places: Libya; Luanda; Middle East; Norway

oil spill
DISCUSSIONS
pollution *volume* **1** *page* **73**, photograph *volume* **1** *page* **72**

Okavango River (river in Africa)
DISCUSSIONS
Botswana *volume* **8** *page* **71**
LEARN MORE *look under* Botswana; rivers

Okefenokee Swamp (swamp in the U.S.)
DISCUSSIONS
swamps *volume* **1** *page* **28**

Old Faithful (geyser in Wyoming, U.S.)
DISCUSSIONS
thermal power photograph *volume* **2** *page* **65**

Old Parliament House (building in Canberra, Australia)
DISCUSSIONS
Canberra *volume* **7** *page* **91**, photograph *volume* **7** *page* **91**

Old Testament (Bible)
DISCUSSIONS
Bible *volume* **5** *page* **63**
Judaism *volume* **5** *page* **50**

Old Town Square (square in Prague, Czech Republic)
DISCUSSIONS
Prague *volume* **6** *page* **55**

Old World porcupines
DISCUSSIONS
porcupines *volume* **12** *page* **70**, photograph *volume* **12** *page* **71**

Oldenburg, Claes (American artist)
DISCUSSIONS
sculpture photograph *volume* **3** *page* **10**

olive
ARTICLE *volume* **10** *page* **61**
DISCUSSIONS
Greece *volume* **6** *page* **83**
LEARN MORE *look under* fruits and vegetables; trees

Olmec (people)
DISCUSSIONS
Mexico *volume* **9** *page* **41**
LEARN MORE *look under* American Indians

Olympic Games
DISCUSSIONS
Athens *volume* **6** *page* **85**
Cathy Freeman *volume* **4** *page* **92**, photograph *volume* **4** *page* **92**, photograph *volume* **4** *page* **93**
Greece *volume* **6** *page* **83**
LEARN MORE *look under* sports

Olympic Peninsula (peninsula in Washington, U.S.)
DISCUSSIONS
peninsulas *volume* **1** *page* **22**

Olympus, Mount (mountain in Greece)
DISCUSSIONS
Greece *volume* **6** *page* **83**
LEARN MORE *look under* mountains

Olympus Mons (volcano on Mars)
DISCUSSIONS
Mars *volume* **2** *page* **35**
LEARN MORE *look under* volcanoes

Oman (country)
ARTICLE *volume* **7** *page* **82**
DISCUSSIONS
atlas *volume* **13** *page* **8**
flag *volume* **7** *page* **82**
LEARN MORE *look under* Arabia; Middle East

Ontario (province in Canada)
ARTICLE *volume* **9** *page* **18**
LEARN MORE *look under* Canada; Great Lakes

Ontario, Lake (lake in North America)
DISCUSSIONS
Great Lakes *volume* **9** *page* **23**
Ontario *volume* **9** *page* **19**
LEARN MORE *look under* North America

oolong tea
DISCUSSIONS
tea *volume* **10** *page* **39**

opera (music)
ARTICLE *volume* **3** *page* **76**
DISCUSSIONS
classical music *volume* **3** *page* **36**

LEARN MORE *look under* music; theatre
people: Mozart, Wolfgang Amadeus;
Sutherland, Joan; Te Kanawa, Kiri

opossums, *also called* possums
(animals)
ARTICLE *volume* **12** *page* **83**
LEARN MORE *look under* marsupials
stories: 'Why Possum's Tail Is Bare'

orang-utans (apes)
DISCUSSIONS
apes *volume* **12** *page* **9,** photograph
volume **12** *page* **8**

orange juice
DISCUSSIONS
oranges *volume* **10** *page* **49**

oranges (fruit)
ARTICLE *volume* **10** *page* **49**
LEARN MORE *look under* fruits and
vegetables; trees

orbit (astronomy)
DISCUSSIONS
asteroids *volume* **2** *page* **22**

orchestra (music)
DISCUSSIONS
classical music *volume* **3** *page* **36,**
photograph *volume* **3** *page* **37**
LEARN MORE *look under* musical
instruments

orchids (plants)
ARTICLE *volume* **10** *page* **17**
LEARN MORE *look under* flowers

Oriental cockroaches (insects)
DISCUSSIONS
cockroaches *volume* **11** *page* **65**
LEARN MORE *look under* insects

Ormazd (Zoroastrian god): *look under*
Ahura Mazda

Orthodox Judaism
DISCUSSIONS
Judaism *volume* **5** *page* **50**

Osage (Native American people)
DISCUSSIONS
Maria Tallchief *volume* **3** *page* **91**
LEARN MORE *look under* American
Indians

ostriches (birds)
ARTICLE *volume* **11** *page* **31**
LEARN MORE *look under* birds; kiwis

Ottawa (city in Canada)
ARTICLE *volume* **9** *page* **14**
DISCUSSIONS
atlas *volume* **13** *page* **14**

outer space: *look under* space

Ovimbundu (people)
DISCUSSIONS
Angola *volume* **8** *page* **67**

owls (birds)
ARTICLE *volume* **11** *page* **13**
LEARN MORE *look under* birds

oxygen (chemical element)
DISCUSSIONS
leaves *volume* **1** *page* **67**

Pacific Ocean
ARTICLE *volume* **1** *page* **41**
DISCUSSIONS
Ferdinand Magellan *volume* **4**
page **101**
Great Barrier Reef *volume* **7** *page* **92**
islands photograph *volume* **1** *page* **12**
Panama City *volume* **9** *page* **50**
LEARN MORE *look under* Easter Island;
Galapagos Islands

Pacific walruses
DISCUSSIONS
walruses *volume* **12** *page* **75**

pagodas (architecture)
DISCUSSIONS
Japan photograph *volume* **7** *page* **15**

painted turtles (animals)
DISCUSSIONS
turtles photograph *volume* **11** *page* **88**

painting (art)
ARTICLE *volume* **3** *page* **8**
LEARN MORE *look under*
people: Goya, Francisco de;
Hiroshige; Kahlo, Frida;
Michelangelo; Picasso, Pablo;
Rivera, Diego; van Gogh, Vincent;
Xia Gui

Pakistan (country)
ARTICLE *volume* **7** *page* **59**
DISCUSSIONS
atlas *volume* **13** *page* **8**
Bangladesh *volume* **7** *page* **47**
flag *volume* **7** *page* **59**
Indus Civilization *volume* **7** *page* **60**
Muslim school photograph *volume* **5**
page **69**

LEARN MORE *look under*
people: Jinnah, Mohammed Ali;
Khan, Nusrat Fateh Ali
places: South Asia
religion: Islam

palaces
DISCUSSIONS
Kathmandu *volume* **7** *page* **56**
Seoul *volume* **7** *page* **23,** photograph
volume **7** *page* **22**
Thailand *volume* **7** *page* **37**
LEARN MORE *look under* architecture
individual palaces: Buckingham
Palace; Chaillot Palace;
Congressional Palace; Forbidden
City; Iolani Palace; Royal Palace;
Schönbrunn Palace

palaeontology (science)
DISCUSSIONS
geology *volume* **1** *page* **75**
LEARN MORE *look under* Cretaceous
Period; fossils

Palestine (region in the Middle East)
DISCUSSIONS
Golda Meir *volume* **4** *page* **57**
Islam photograph *volume* **5** *page* **64**
Isreal *volume* **7** *page* **75**
Menachem Begin *volume* **4** *page* **35**
Yasir Arafat *volume* **4** *page* **30,**
photograph *volume* **4** *page* **31**
LEARN MORE *look under* Israel; Middle
East

Palestine Liberation Organization,
also called PLO
DISCUSSIONS
Yasir Arafat *volume* **4** *page* **30**

Palm Pilot (computer)
DISCUSSIONS
handheld computers photograph
volume **2** *page* **79**

palms
ARTICLE *volume* **10** *page* **45**
DISCUSSIONS
date palms photograph *volume* **1**
page **35**
LEARN MORE *look under* trees

Pampas, the (grasslands in Argentina)
DISCUSSIONS
Argentina *volume* **9** *page* **90**
LEARN MORE *look under* grasses

'Pan American Unity' (mural by
Rivera)
DISCUSSIONS
Diego Rivera illustration *volume* **3**
page **22**

Panama (country)
DISCUSSIONS
flag *volume* **9** *page* **50**
Panama Canal *volume* **9** *page* **52**
LEARN MORE *look under*
places: Central America; Panama
City

Panama Canal (canal in Central
America)
ARTICLE *volume* **9** *page* **52**
DISCUSSIONS
atlas *volume* **13** *page* **14**
Panama City *volume* **9** *page* **50**
LEARN MORE *look under* canals; Central
America; Panama City

Panama City (city in Panama)
ARTICLE *volume* **9** *page* **50**
DISCUSSIONS
atlas *volume* **13** *page* **14**
LEARN MORE *look under* Panama;
Panama Canal

pandas (animals)
ARTICLE *volume* **12** *page* **38**
LEARN MORE *look under* carnivores

paper
ARTICLE *volume* **2** *page* **87**
DISCUSSIONS
rushes and reeds *volume* **10** *page* **65**
LEARN MORE *look under* printing; trees

paper mills
DISCUSSIONS
paper *volume* **2** *page* **87**, photograph
volume **2** *page* **86**

paprika (plant)
DISCUSSIONS
peppers *volume* **10** *page* **34**

Papua New Guinea (country)
DISCUSSIONS
tsunamis *volume* **1** *page* **50**
yams photograph *volume* **10** *page* **32**
LEARN MORE *look under* Southeast Asia

papyruses (plants)
DISCUSSIONS
rushes and reeds *volume* **10** *page* **65**

Paraguay (country)
ARTICLE *volume* **9** *page* **83**
DISCUSSIONS
atlas *volume* **13** *page* **17**
Asunción *volume* **9** *page* **85**
flag *volume* **9** *page* **83**
LEARN MORE *look under*
places: South America
animals: armadillos; bats; monkeys

Paris (city in France)
ARTICLE *volume* **6** *page* **35**

DISCUSSIONS
atlas *volume* **13** *page* **6**
France photograph *volume* **6** *page* **32**
LEARN MORE *look under*
places: Bucharest; Eiffel Tower;
France; Louvre

parks: *look under* Banff National Park;
Beihai Park; Central Park; Etosha
National Park; Glacier Bay National
Park; Hwange National Park; Mount
Rushmore National Memorial; National
Botanic Gardens; Phoenix Park

Parliament, Houses of (buildings in
London, England, U.K.)
DISCUSSIONS
London *volume* **6** *page* **16**

Parliament House (building in
Canberra, Australia)
DISCUSSIONS
Canberra *volume* **7** *page* **91**

Parliament House (building in Perth,
Australia)
DISCUSSIONS
Western Australia photograph
volume **7** *page* **96**

parrots and cockatoos (birds)
ARTICLE *volume* **11** *page* **11**
DISCUSSIONS
Amazon photograph *volume* **9**
page **65**
LEARN MORE *look under* Amazon
parrot; birds

Parsis (people)
DISCUSSIONS
Zoroastrianism *volume* **5** *page* **49**,
photograph *volume* **5** *page* **48**
LEARN MORE *look under* India; peoples

Parson's chameleons (lizards)
DISCUSSIONS
chameleons photograph *volume* **11**
page **86**

Parthenon (temple in Greece)
ARTICLE *volume* **6** *page* **87**
LEARN MORE *look under* Athens;
temples

passenger pigeons (birds)
DISCUSSIONS
Did you know? *volume* **9** *page* **26**
LEARN MORE *look under* birds

pasta (food)
DISCUSSIONS
Did you know? *volume* **7** *page* **9**
LEARN MORE *look under* food

Pasteur, Louis (French scientist)
ARTICLE *volume* **4** *page* **85**
LEARN MORE *look under*
people: Curie, Marie
things: medicine; science

pasteurization
DISCUSSIONS
Louis Pasteur *volume* **4** *page* **85**

Patagonia (region in Argentina)
DISCUSSIONS
Argentina *volume* **9** *page* **90**,
photograph *volume* **9** *page* **91**

patas monkeys (animals)
DISCUSSIONS
monkeys photograph *volume* **12**
page **14**

'Pather Panchali' (film by Ray)
DISCUSSIONS
Satyajit Ray *volume* **3** *page* **89**

'Paula' (book by Allende)
DISCUSSIONS
Isabel Allende *volume* **4** *page* **7**

PC (computer): *look under* personal
computers

peacocks (birds)
ARTICLE *volume* **11** *page* **28**
LEARN MORE *look under* birds

peanuts
ARTICLE *volume* **10** *page* **30**
DISCUSSIONS
nuts *volume* **10** *page* **59**
LEARN MORE *look under* fruits and
vegetables; plants

Pearl Harbor (naval base in Hawaii,
U.S.)
DISCUSSIONS
Honolulu *volume* **9** *page* **35**

peat moss (plant)
DISCUSSIONS
mosses *volume* **10** *page* **87**
LEARN MORE *look under* mosses

Pei, I. M., *also called* Ieoh Ming Pei
(Chinese-American architect)
ARTICLE *volume* **4** *page* **18**
LEARN MORE *look under* architecture
other architects: Fathy, Hassan;
Michelangelo

Peking (city in China): *look under*
Beijing

Peking opera, *also called* jingxi
DISCUSSIONS
opera *volume* **3** *page* **76**, photograph
volume **3** *page* **77**

Pelé, *also called* Edson Arantes do Nascimento (Brazilian athlete)
ARTICLE *volume* **4** *page* **104**
DISCUSSIONS
Brazil *volume* **9** *page* **79**
LEARN MORE *look under* sports

penguins (birds)
ARTICLE *volume* **11** *page* **27**
DISCUSSIONS
Antarctica *volume* **1** *page* **11**
LEARN MORE *look under* birds; marine animals

penicillin (drug)
DISCUSSIONS
medicine *volume* **2** *page* **60**

peninsulas
ARTICLE *volume* **1** *page* **22**
LEARN MORE *look under*
places: Italy; Korean Peninsula
similar things: islands

Pentateuch (sacred text): *look under* Torah

peoples: *look under*
Africa: Berbers; Boers; Fulani; Herero; Malagasy; Masai; Mbundu; Ndebele; Tswana; Wolof; Yoruba; Zulu
Americas: African Americans; American Indians; Inuit; Ladino
Asia, Australia, and New Zealand: Arabs; Australian Aboriginals; Canaanites; Israel; Khmer; Maori; Parsis; Sherpas; Sumerians
Europe: Franks; Vikings

peppers (plants)
ARTICLE *volume* **10** *page* **34**
LEARN MORE *look under* fruits and vegetables

perching ducks (birds)
DISCUSSIONS
ducks *volume* **11** *page* **21**

percussion instruments (music): *look under* rhythm instruments

performing arts: *look under* cinema; dance; opera; theatre

periscopes (viewing devices)
DISCUSSIONS
submarines *volume* **2** *page* **99**

Persia (country): *look under* Iran

personal computers, *also called* PC
DISCUSSIONS
computers *volume* **2** *page* **79**

Perth (city in Australia)
DISCUSSIONS
atlas *volume* **13** *page* **10**
Western Australia *volume* **7** *page* **97**, photograph *volume* **7** *page* **96**

Peru (country)
ARTICLE *volume* **9** *page* **75**
DISCUSSIONS
atlas *volume* **13** *page* **17**
Amazon *volume* **9** *page* **62**, map *volume* **9** *page* **63**
flag *volume* **9** *page* **75**
llamas photograph *volume* **12** *page* **62**, photograph *volume* **12** *page* **63**
LEARN MORE *look under*
people: Bolívar, Simón
places: South America
animals: alpacas; llamas

Pest (former town in Hungary): *look under* Budapest

petrol (fuel)
DISCUSSIONS
oil *volume* **2** *page* **84**

petroleum: *look under* oil

petrology (science)
DISCUSSIONS
geology *volume* **1** *page* **75**

pharaohs (Egyptian kings)
DISCUSSIONS
Did you know? *volume* **5** *page* **44**
Egypt *volume* **8** *page* **49**
wheat *volume* **10** *page* **75**

Philippines (country)
ARTICLE *volume* **7** *page* **33**
DISCUSSIONS
atlas *volume* **13** *page* **8**
Ferdinand Magellan *volume* **4** *page* **101**
flag *volume* **7** *page* **33**
LEARN MORE *look under* Southeast Asia

Phnom Penh (city in Cambodia)
ARTICLE *volume* **7** *page* **24**
DISCUSSIONS
atlas *volume* **13** *page* **8**
LEARN MORE *look under* Southeast Asia

Phoenix Park (park in Dublin, Ireland)
DISCUSSIONS
Dublin *volume* **6** *page* **26**

photography
ARTICLE *volume* **2** *page* **88**
DISCUSSIONS
motion pictures *volume* **2** *page* **82**
LEARN MORE *look under* communications; motion pictures

photosynthesis (biology)
DISCUSSIONS
energy *volume* **2** *page* **48**
leaves *volume* **1** *page* **67**

physical sciences: *look under* astronomy; atoms; Earth; electricity; energy; gravity; liquids, solids, and gases; measurement; medicine; nuclear energy; technology; temperatures; thermal power; water power; wind power

piano
DISCUSSIONS
Ludwig van Beethoven *volume* **3** *page* **40**

Piazzi, Giuseppe (Italian astronomer)
DISCUSSIONS
asteroids *volume* **2** *page* **22**
LEARN MORE *look under* astronomy
other astronomers: Copernicus, Nicolaus; Galileo Galilei; Kepler, Johannes

Picasso, Pablo (Spanish artist)
ARTICLE *volume* **4** *page* **20**
LEARN MORE *look under* painting; sculpture

'Pietà' (painting by Morales)
DISCUSSIONS
Mary illustration *volume* **5** *page* **61**

'Pietà' (sculpture by Michelangelo): *look under* 'Madonna della Pietà'

pigs
ARTICLE *volume* **12** *page* **64**
LEARN MORE *look under* farming; ungulates

Pillar Edicts (inscriptions by Ashoka): *look under* Rock Edicts

Pillars of Islam
DISCUSSIONS
Islam *volume* **5** *page* **64**

pimientos (plants)
DISCUSSIONS
peppers *volume* **10** *page* **34**

pines (trees)
ARTICLE *volume* **10** *page* **89**
LEARN MORE *look under* trees

pipelines
DISCUSSIONS
oil *volume* **2** *page* **84**

piranhas (fish)
ARTICLE *volume* **11** *page* **41**
DISCUSSIONS
Amazon *volume* **9** *page* **64**

LEARN MORE *look under* fish

pirate spiders
DISCUSSIONS
spiders *volume* **11** *page* **72**

pirates
DISCUSSIONS
Did you know? *volume* **9** *page* **54**

pistachios
DISCUSSIONS
nuts *volume* **10** *page* **59**
LEARN MORE *look under* nuts

pitcher plant
DISCUSSIONS
carnivorous plants *volume* **10** *page* **19**

plains
DISCUSSIONS
grasses photograph *volume* **10** *page* **63**

plains buffalo: *look under* bison

Plains Indians
DISCUSSIONS
American Indians *volume* **4** *page* **87**

planets
ARTICLE *volume* **2** *page* **28**
DISCUSSIONS
solar system *volume* **2** *page* **21**
LEARN MORE *look under*
planets in our solar system: Earth; Jupiter; Mars; Mercury; Neptune; Pluto; Saturn; Uranus; Venus
other things: asteroids; space

plants
DISCUSSIONS
fossilized fern photograph *volume* **1** *page* **84**
leaves *volume* **1** *page* **67**
Luther Burbank *volume* **4** *page* **66**
medicine *volume* **2** *page* **60**
rainforests *volume* **1** *page* **24**
LEARN MORE *look under* cactus; cotton; flowering plants; flowers; fossils; fruits and vegetables; grasses; heath; mosses; trees

Plato (Greek philosopher)
DISCUSSIONS
Socrates *volume* **4** *page* **24**

platypuses (animals)
ARTICLE *volume* **12** *page* **84**
LEARN MORE *look under* mammals
other Australian animals: kangaroos; koalas

plays (literature and performance): *look under* drama

playwrights
DISCUSSIONS
theatre *volume* **3** *page* **72**
LEARN MORE *look under* Shakespeare, William; Soyinka, Wole

PLO (Palestinian political organization): *look under* Palestine Liberation Organization

Pluto (Disney character)
DISCUSSIONS
Did you know? *volume* **2** *page* **45**

Pluto (planet)
ARTICLE *volume* **2** *page* **45**
DISCUSSIONS
Did you know? *volume* **2** *page* **7**
planets *volume* **2** *page* **28**
solar system *volume* **2** *page* **21**, illustration *volume* **2** *page* **20**

poetry: *look under*
people: Basho; Brooks, Gwendolyn; Dickinson, Emily; Tagore, Rabindranath; Walker, Kath
things: qawwali

Point Xaafuun (coastal feature of Somalia)
DISCUSSIONS
Did you know? *volume* **8** *page* **37**

Poland (country)
ARTICLE *volume* **6** *page* **57**
DISCUSSIONS
atlas *volume* **13** *page* **6**
flag *volume* **6** *page* **57**
LEARN MORE *look under*
people: Copernicus, Nicolaus
places: Central Europe

polar bears
DISCUSSIONS
Did you know? *volume* **9** *page* **11**
mammals photograph *volume* **12** *page* **6**
LEARN MORE *look under* carnivores

polders (reclaimed land)
DISCUSSIONS
Netherlands, the *volume* **6** *page* **38**

police
DISCUSSIONS
dogs photograph *volume* **12** *page* **29**

pollination
DISCUSSIONS
bats *volume* **12** *page* **89**
Luther Burbank *volume* **4** *page* **66**

polliwogs (animals): *look under* tadpoles

pollution
ARTICLE *volume* **1** *page* **73**

DISCUSSIONS
Atlantic Ocean *volume* **1** *page* **39**
Great Lakes *volume* **9** *page* **23**
nuclear energy *volume* **2** *page* **62**
LEARN MORE *look under* acid rain; recycling

Polyphemus (Greek legend)
DISCUSSIONS
Greek legend *volume* **5** *page* **27**

polytheism
DISCUSSIONS
God *volume* **5** *page* **44**

Pompeii (ancient city in Italy)
DISCUSSIONS
dogs *volume* **12** *page* **29**
volcanoes *volume* **1** *page* **15**

Pompey the Great (Roman statesman)
DISCUSSIONS
Julius Caesar *volume* **4** *page* **37**

pond skaters (insects)
DISCUSSIONS
insects *volume* **11** *page* **57**

'Poor Man and the Flask of Oil, The' (South Asian folktale)
ARTICLE *volume* **5** *page* **18**
LEARN MORE *look under*
other Asian stories: Moni Mekhala and Ream Eyso; 'Tiger in the Trap, The'; 'Yeh-Shen'
other folktales: 'Ananse and the Wisdom Pot'; 'How Kangaroo Got His Tail'; 'Monkey Court, The'; 'Rabbit Throws Away His Sandal'

popular music, *also called* pop music
ARTICLE *volume* **3** *page* **32**
LEARN MORE *look under*
people: Santana, Carlos
things: folk music; jazz; Ladysmith Black Mambazo

porcupines
ARTICLE *volume* **12** *page* **70**
LEARN MORE *look under* muskrats; rabbits and hares; raccoons

'Portrait of Dr. Gachet' (painting by van Gogh)
DISCUSSIONS
Did you know? *volume* **3** *page* **26**

portraits (art)
DISCUSSIONS
Francisco de Goya illustration *volume* **4** *page* **14**
Frida Kahlo *volume* **3** *page* **19**, illustration *volume* **3** *page* **18**
painting *volume* **3** *page* **8**

'Ran' (film by Kurosawa)
DISCUSSIONS
Akira Kurosawa photograph
volume **3** *page* **86**

Rangoon (city in Myanmar): *look under*
Yangon

rap music
DISCUSSIONS
Did you know? *volume* **3** *page* **30**

Ray, Satyajit (Indian film director)
ARTICLE *volume* **3** *page* **89**
DISCUSSIONS
Ravi Shankar *volume* **3** *page* **48**
LEARN MORE *look under* motion
pictures

realism (art)
DISCUSSIONS
Francisco de Goya *volume* **4** *page* **14**
LEARN MORE *look under* painting

Ream Eyso (Cambodian myth): *look
under* Moni Mekhala and Ream Eyso

receiver
DISCUSSIONS
telephones *volume* **2** *page* **100**

recycling
DISCUSSIONS
Did you know? *volume* **1** *page* **72**
paper *volume* **2** *page* **87**

red bear cats: *look under* lesser pandas

red-bellied piranhas
DISCUSSIONS
piranhas *volume* **11** *page* **41**
LEARN MORE *look under* fish

red planet: *look under* Mars

Red Sea (sea in the Middle East)
DISCUSSIONS
Suez Canal *volume* **8** *page* **56**

red wolves
DISCUSSIONS
wolves *volume* **12** *page* **31**

reeds (plants): *look under* rushes and
reeds

reefs: *look under* Great Barrier Reef

refineries (oil)
DISCUSSIONS
oil *volume* **2** *page* **84**

Reform Judaism
DISCUSSIONS
Judaism *volume* **5** *page* **50**

reincarnation
DISCUSSIONS
Dalai Lama *volume* **5** *page* **85**
Hinduism *volume* **5** *page* **79**
Sikhism *volume* **5** *page* **88**

relativity (science)
DISCUSSIONS
Albert Einstein *volume* **4** *page* **74**

religion
ARTICLE *volume* **5** *page* **42**
DISCUSSIONS
calendars *volume* **2** *page* **77**
dance *volume* **3** *page* **70**
Did you know? *volume* **5** *page* **82**,
volume **7** *page* **6**
folk arts and crafts *volume* **3** *page* **6**
LEARN MORE *look under*
religion: Baha'i; Buddhism;
Christianity; Daoism; Hinduism;
Islam; Jainism; Judaism;
shamanism; Shinto; Sikhism;
Vodun; Zoroastrianism
people: Abraham; Buddha;
Confucius; Dalai Lama; God; Jesus
Christ; Mary; Moses; Muhammad
other things: Bible; Koran;
monasticism

Renaissance (European history)
DISCUSSIONS
Michelangelo photograph *volume* **3**
page **20**

reptiles (animals)
ARTICLE *volume* **11** *page* **74**
LEARN MORE *look under* alligators and
crocodiles; anacondas; chameleons;
dinosaurs; iguanas; king cobras;
lizards; snakes; turtles

Republic of the Congo (country)
DISCUSSIONS
atlas *volume* **13** *page* **12**
Congo region *volume* **8** *page* **9**
flag *volume* **8** *page* **9**
LEARN MORE *look under* Congo

reservation, Indian: *look under* Indian
reservations

resins (chemicals)
DISCUSSIONS
pines *volume* **10** *page* **89**
LEARN MORE *look under* trees

resurrection (religion)
DISCUSSIONS
Jesus Christ *volume* **5** *page* **58**
Koran *volume* **5** *page* **69**

Revelation, Book of (New Testament)
DISCUSSIONS
Bible *volume* **5** *page* **63**

'Revelations' (dance by Ailey)
DISCUSSIONS
Alvin Ailey *volume* **3** *page* **78**,
photograph *volume* **3** *page* **79**

Reykjavik (city in Iceland)
ARTICLE *volume* **6** *page* **59**
DISCUSSIONS
atlas *volume* **13** *page* **6**
thermal power *volume* **2** *page* **64**
LEARN MORE *look under* Iceland;
Scandinavia; Vikings

Rh factor (blood)
DISCUSSIONS
macaques *volume* **12** *page* **17**

rhesus monkeys (animals)
DISCUSSIONS
macaques *volume* **12** *page* **17**,
photograph *volume* **12** *page* **17**

Rhodes, Cecil (British leader)
DISCUSSIONS
Zimbabwe *volume* **8** *page* **89**

rhythm instruments
DISCUSSIONS
Count Basie *volume* **4** *page* **9**

rice
ARTICLE *volume* **10** *page* **73**
DISCUSSIONS
China *volume* **7** *page* **8**, photograph
volume **7** *page* **9**
marshes *volume* **1** *page* **26**
Vietnam photograph *volume* **7**
page **41**
LEARN MORE *look under* grasses

'Rikki-Tikki-Tavi' (story by Kipling)
DISCUSSIONS
Did you know? *volume* **12** *page* **37**

ring-tailed lemurs (mammals)
DISCUSSIONS
lemurs *volume* **12** *page* **19**,
photograph *volume* **12** *page* **19**

ringtails (animals): *look under* raccoons

Rio de Janeiro (city in Brazil)
DISCUSSIONS
atlas *volume* **13** *page* **17**
Brazil *volume* **9** *page* **79**, photograph
volume **9** *page* **78**
Did you know? *volume* **6** *page* **9**

Rivera, Diego (Mexican painter)
ARTICLE *volume* **3** *page* **22**
DISCUSSIONS
Frida Kahlo *volume* **3** *page* **19**

LEARN MORE *look under* painting

rivers
ARTICLE *volume* **1** *page* **30**
DISCUSSIONS
sand *volume* **1** *page* **18**
swamps *volume* **1** *page* **28**
LEARN MORE *look under*
rivers: Amazon; Colorado River;
Congo River; Danube; Ganges
River; Liffey, River; Mackenzie
River; Mississippi River; Nile River;
Okavango River; Sava River; Seine
River; Vltava River; Yangtze River;
Zambezi River
animals: alligators and crocodiles;
carp; fish; hippopotamuses;
manatees; piranhas
things: floods; glaciers; waterways

rock (music): *look under* rock music

rock and roll (music): *look under* rock music

Rock Edicts (inscriptions by Ashoka)
DISCUSSIONS
Ashoka *volume* **4** *page* **32**

rock music, *also called* rock and roll
LEARN MORE *look under*
people: Santana, Carlos

rockets
DISCUSSIONS
astronauts *volume* **2** *page* **19,**
photograph *volume* **2** *page* **18**
LEARN MORE *look under* technology

Rocks, The (district in Sydney, Australia)
DISCUSSIONS
Sydney *volume* **7** *page* **95,**
photograph *volume* **7** *page* **95**

rocks and minerals
ARTICLE *volume* **1** *page* **76**
DISCUSSIONS
Did you know? *volume* **1** *page* **74**
volcanoes *volume* **1** *page* **15**
LEARN MORE *look under* chalk;
diamonds; fossils; sand

rodents (animals)
DISCUSSIONS
owls *volume* **11** *page* **13**
LEARN MORE *look under* muskrats;
porcupines

Rodin, Auguste (French sculptor)
ARTICLE *volume* **3** *page* **24**
LEARN MORE *look under* sculpture
people: Michelangelo; Picasso, Pablo

Roman Catholicism (religion)
DISCUSSIONS
Christianity *volume* **5** *page* **57**
Did you know? *volume* **4** *page* **76,**
volume **9** *page* **84**
Guatemala *volume* **9** *page* **46**
Mary *volume* **5** *page* **61**
Poland *volume* **6** *page* **57**
religion photograph *volume* **5** *page* **43**
Vatican City *volume* **6** *page* **93**
Vodun *volume* **5** *page* **92**
LEARN MORE *look under* Christianity;
monasticism
people: Abraham; Jesus Christ;
Moses; Teresa, Mother

Roman Forum (area in Rome, Italy)
DISCUSSIONS
Rome *volume* **6** *page* **91,** photograph
volume **6** *page* **90**

Roman Republic and Empire
DISCUSSIONS
Did you know? *volume* **12** *page* **90**
God *volume* **5** *page* **44**
Rome *volume* **6** *page* **91**
sponges *volume* **11** *page* **47**
Tripoli *volume* **8** *page* **61**
LEARN MORE *look under*
people: Caesar, Julius
things: Byzantine Empire

Romania (country)
DISCUSSIONS
atlas *volume* **13** *page* **6**
flag *volume* **6** *page* **73**
LEARN MORE *look under*
places: Bucharest; Eastern Europe

Romanticism (arts)
DISCUSSIONS
Did you know? *volume* **3** *page* **41**
LEARN MORE *look under* literature;
music

Rome (city in Italy)
ARTICLE *volume* **6** *page* **91**
DISCUSSIONS
atlas *volume* **13** *page* **6**
Italy *volume* **6** *page* **89,** photograph
volume **6** *page* **89**
LEARN MORE *look under* Vatican City

roses
ARTICLE *volume* **10** *page* **11**
LEARN MORE *look under* flowers

Rossini, Gioacchino (Italian composer)
DISCUSSIONS
opera *volume* **3** *page* **76**

Round Table (British legend): *look under* Knights of the Round Table

Royal Palace (palace in Phnom Penh, Cambodia)
DISCUSSIONS
Phnom Penh photograph *volume* **7** *page* **25**
LEARN MORE *look under* palaces

rubber trees
ARTICLE *volume* **10** *page* **90**
LEARN MORE *look under* trees

Rubicon (stream in Italy)
DISCUSSIONS
Caesar photograph *volume* **4** *page* **36**

Ruby Marshes (marsh in Nevada, U.S.)
DISCUSSIONS
marshes photograph *volume* **1** *page* **27**

ruminants (animals)
DISCUSSIONS
cattle *volume* **12** *page* **47**

running (sports): *look under* Freeman, Cathy

rushes and reeds (plants)
ARTICLE *volume* **10** *page* **65**
LEARN MORE *look under* grasses

Rushmore, Mount (monument in South Dakota, U.S): *look under* Mount Rushmore National Memorial

Ruska, Kathleen Jean Mary (Australian writer): *look under* Walker, Kath

Russia (country)
ARTICLE *volume* **6** *page* **69**
DISCUSSIONS
atlas *volume* **13** *page* **6,** *volume* **13** *page* **8**
astronauts *volume* **2** *page* **19**
flag *volume* **6** *page* **69**
LEARN MORE *look under* Northern
Europe; Union of Soviet Socialist
Republics

Rwanda (country)
DISCUSSIONS
atlas *volume* **13** *page* **12**
gorillas photograph *volume* **12** *page* **11**
LEARN MORE *look under* Africa

sabi (Japanese art)
DISCUSSIONS
Did you know? *volume* **3** *page* **53**

sacred kingfishers (birds)
DISCUSSIONS
kingfishers photograph *volume* **11** *page* **9**

sacred writings: *look under* 'Adi Granth'; Avesta; Bible; 'Daodejing'; Koran

Sadat, Anwar el- (Egyptian leader)
ARTICLE *volume* **4** *page* **59**
DISCUSSIONS
Menachem Begin *volume* **4** *page* **35**
LEARN MORE *look under* Egypt
other Middle Eastern leaders: Arafat, Yasir; Meir, Golda

Sadat Resthouse (building in Egypt)
DISCUSSIONS
Hassan Fathy photograph *volume* **3** *page* **14**
LEARN MORE *look under* architecture; Egypt

saddles (horseback riding)
DISCUSSIONS
horses photograph *volume* **12** *page* **41**

Sagarmatha (mountain in Asia): *look under* Everest, Mount

Sahara (desert in Africa)
DISCUSSIONS
atlas *volume* **13** *page* **12**
Africa *volume* **8** *page* **7**
Algeria *volume* **8** *page* **44**, photograph *volume* **8** *page* **45**
Libya *volume* **8** *page* **58**
oasis *volume* **1** *page* **34**, photograph *volume* **1** *page* **35**
LEARN MORE *look under* deserts

Sahel (region in Africa)
DISCUSSIONS
Did you know? *volume* **4** *page* **72**

sailing ships
DISCUSSIONS
ships *volume* **2** *page* **94**

Saint Basil's Cathedral (church in Russia)
DISCUSSIONS
Russia photograph *volume* **6** *page* **68**

Saint Peter's Basilica (church in Vatican City)
DISCUSSIONS
religion photograph *volume* **5** *page* **43**
Vatican City *volume* **6** *page* **93**, photograph *volume* **6** *page* **92**

Saint Stephen's Cathedral (church in Vienna, Austria)
DISCUSSIONS
Vienna *volume* **6** *page* **51**

salamanders (animals)
DISCUSSIONS
amphibians *volume* **11** *page* **91**

salmon (fish)
ARTICLE *volume* **11** *page* **39**
LEARN MORE *look under* fish

Salt March (Indian history)
DISCUSSIONS
Mahatma Gandhi *volume* **4** *page* **95**

salt marshes
DISCUSSIONS
marshes *volume* **1** *page* **26**

salties (animals)
DISCUSSIONS
Did you know? *volume* **11** *page* **77**

Salzburg (city in Austria)
DISCUSSIONS
Austria *volume* **6** *page* **48**, photograph *volume* **6** *page* **49**

San Juan (city in Puerto Rico)
DISCUSSIONS
Puerto Rico photograph *volume* **9** *page* **56**

sand
ARTICLE *volume* **1** *page* **18**
DISCUSSIONS
Did you know? *volume* **1** *page* **21**
LEARN MORE *look under* rocks and minerals

sand dunes
DISCUSSIONS
sand photograph *volume* **1** *page* **18**

sand painting
DISCUSSIONS
painting *volume* **3** *page* **8**, photograph *volume* **3** *page* **8**

sandstone (rock)
DISCUSSIONS
canyons photograph *volume* **1** *page* **76**, photograph *volume* **1** *page* **77**

Santana, Carlos (Mexican-American musician)
ARTICLE *volume* **3** *page* **47**

LEARN MORE *look under* popular music

Santiago (city in Chile)
DISCUSSIONS
Chile *volume* **9** *page* **87**
LEARN MORE *look under* South America

Sarah (biblical person)
DISCUSSIONS
Abraham *volume* **5** *page* **52**

Sargassum (seaweed)
DISCUSSIONS
seaweed *volume* **10** *page* **93**

sari (clothing)
DISCUSSIONS
Did you know? *volume* **4** *page* **107**

Sarnath (archaeological site in India)
DISCUSSIONS
Ashoka photograph *volume* **4** *page* **33**

Satchmo (American musician): *look under* Armstrong, Louis

satellites (objects in space)
DISCUSSIONS
spacecraft *volume* **2** *page* **16**
television *volume* **2** *page* **104**

Saturn (planet)
ARTICLE *volume* **2** *page* **39**
DISCUSSIONS
solar system illustration *volume* **2** *page* **20**
LEARN MORE *look under* planets

satyagraha (non-violence)
DISCUSSIONS
Did you know? *volume* **4** *page* **95**

Saudi Arabia (country)
DISCUSSIONS
atlas *volume* **13** *page* **8**
Did you know? *volume* **5** *page* **65**
oasis *volume* **1** *page* **34**
LEARN MORE *look under* Mecca

Sava River (river in Europe)
DISCUSSIONS
Belgrade photograph *volume* **6** *page* **79**
LEARN MORE *look under* rivers

savannahs (grasslands)
DISCUSSIONS
Guinea *volume* **8** *page* **14**, photograph *volume* **8** *page* **15**
Nigeria *volume* **8** *page* **20**

saw-whet owls, *also called* Aegolius acadicus (birds)
DISCUSSIONS
owls photograph *volume* **11** *page* **13**

skinks (reptiles)
DISCUSSIONS
lizards photograph *volume* **11** *page* **85**

slavery
DISCUSSIONS
Cuba *volume* **9** *page* **59**
Dakar *volume* **8** *page* **25**
Liberia *volume* **8** *page* **17**
Monrovia *volume* **8** *page* **19**
Senegal *volume* **8** *page* **23**
West Indies *volume* **9** *page* **54**

Slotsholmen (island in Denmark)
DISCUSSIONS
Copenhagen *volume* **6** *page* **62**

smog (air pollution)
DISCUSSIONS
pollution *volume* **1** *page* **73**

snails (animals)
DISCUSSIONS
molluscs photograph *volume* **11** *page* **49**

snake pits
DISCUSSIONS
Did you know? *volume* **11** *page* **79**

snakes (animals)
ARTICLE *volume* **11** *page* **78**
DISCUSSIONS
Ireland *volume* **6** *page* **24**
mongooses *volume* **12** *page* **36**, photograph *volume* **12** *page* **37**
South America photograph *volume* **9** *page* **60**
LEARN MORE *look under* anacondas; cobras; emerald tree boa; king cobras; reptiles

snapdragons (flowers)
DISCUSSIONS
Golden desert variety photograph *volume* **1** *page* **20**
LEARN MORE *look under* flowers

snow (weather)
DISCUSSIONS
clouds *volume* **1** *page* **56**

snow geese (birds)
DISCUSSIONS
geese *volume* **11** *page* **22**, photograph *volume* **11** *page* **22**

snowfield (glacier)
DISCUSSIONS
glaciers *volume* **1** *page* **54**

soccer (sport): *look under* football

social dances
DISCUSSIONS
dance *volume* **3** *page* **70**

Socrates (Greek philosopher)
ARTICLE *volume* **4** *page* **24**

Socratic method (education)
DISCUSSIONS
Socrates *volume* **4** *page* **24**

Sofia, *also called* Serdica, *or* Sredets (city in Bulgaria)
ARTICLE *volume* **6** *page* **74**
DISCUSSIONS
atlas *volume* **13** *page* **6**
LEARN MORE *look under* Eastern Europe

software (computer science)
DISCUSSIONS
computers *volume* **2** *page* **79**

solar energy
DISCUSSIONS
thermal power *volume* **2** *page* **64**

solar oven
DISCUSSIONS
thermal power photograph *volume* **2** *page* **64**

solar system
ARTICLE *volume* **2** *page* **21**
DISCUSSIONS
Johannes Kepler *volume* **4** *page* **81**
Nicolaus Copernicus *volume* **4** *page* **69**, illustration *volume* **4** *page* **69**
LEARN MORE *look under* asteroids; comets; Earth; Jupiter; Mars; Mercury; Neptune; planets; Pluto; Saturn; Uranus; Venus

solids (state of matter): *look under* liquids, solids, and gases

Somalia (country)
ARTICLE *volume* **8** *page* **36**
DISCUSSIONS
atlas *volume* **13** *page* **12**
flag *volume* **8** *page* **36**
LEARN MORE *look under*
places: Eastern Africa; Mogadishu

sonar
DISCUSSIONS
echoes *volume* **1** *page* **69**
submarines *volume* **2** *page* **99**

sonatas (music)
DISCUSSIONS
classical music *volume* **3** *page* **36**

sopranos (music)
DISCUSSIONS
Joan Sutherland *volume* **4** *page* **27**
Kiri Te Kanawa *volume* **3** *page* **92**

soul
DISCUSSIONS
shamanism *volume* **5** *page* **91**
Zoroastrianism *volume* **5** *page* **49**

sound
DISCUSSIONS
echoes *volume* **1** *page* **68**

South Africa (country)
ARTICLE *volume* **8** *page* **82**
DISCUSSIONS
atlas *volume* **13** *page* **12**
chameleons photograph *volume* **11** *page* **87**
cities *volume* **8** *page* **87**
diamonds *volume* **1** *page* **80**
flag *volume* **8** *page* **82**
history *volume* **8** *page* **85**
Namibia *volume* **8** *page* **78**
popular music photograph *volume* **3** *page* **33**
LEARN MORE *look under* Southern Africa
music: Ladysmith Black Mambazo
people: Mandela, Nelson

South America (continent)
ARTICLE *volume* **9** *page* **61**
DISCUSSIONS
atlas *volume* **13** *page* **17**
anacondas *volume* **11** *page* **81**
Andes *volume* **9** *page* **66**
continents *volume* **1** *page* **8**, map *volume* **1** *page* **8**
rainforests *volume* **1** *page* **24**, photograph *volume* **1** *page* **24**
LEARN MORE *look under*
countries: Argentina; Brazil; Chile; Colombia; Paraguay; Peru
other places: Amazon; Andes; Easter Island; Galapagos Islands; Machu Picchu
people: American Indians; Bolívar, Simón
animals: anoles; armadillos; bats; donkeys; llamas; manatees; monkeys; ocelots; opossums; piranhas; porcupines; raccoons; tapirs

South Asia: *look under*
places: Afghanistan; Bangladesh; Dhaka; India; Karakoram Range; Kathmandu; Nepal; Pakistan; Sri Lanka; Taj Mahal; Thimphu
religion: Buddhism; Hinduism; Islam; Jainism; Sikhism; Zoroastrianism
animals: buffalo; camels; elephants; king cobras; mongooses; pandas; wild goats; yaks

'Tom Sawyer' (book by Twain)
DISCUSSIONS
Mark Twain *volume* **4** *page* **29**

tomatoes
ARTICLE *volume* **10** *page* **23**
LEARN MORE *look under* fruits and vegetables

Tonkin (city in Vietnam): *look under* Hanoi

Tonquin (city in Vietnam): *look under* Hanoi

Torah, *also called* Five Books of Moses, *or* Law, *or* Pentateuch (sacred text)
DISCUSSIONS
Bible *volume* **5** *page* **63,** photograph *volume* **5** *page* **63**
Judaism *volume* **5** *page* **50,** photograph *volume* **5** *page* **51**
Moses *volume* **5** *page* **54**

tornadoes (wind storms)
ARTICLE *volume* **1** *page* **61**
LEARN MORE *look under* weather

Toronto (city in Canada)
DISCUSSIONS
atlas *volume* **13** *page* **14**
Canada *volume* **9** *page* **10**
Ontario *volume* **9** *page* **18**
theatre photograph *volume* **3** *page* **73**

Torre, Mount (mountain in Argentina)
DISCUSSIONS
Andes photograph *volume* **9** *page* **67**
LEARN MORE *look under* mountains

tortoises, *also called* land turtles (reptiles)
DISCUSSIONS
Galapagos Islands *volume* **9** *page* **68,** photograph *volume* **9** *page* **69**
turtles *volume* **11** *page* **88**

totem pole
DISCUSSIONS
North America photograph *volume* **9** *page* **6**
LEARN MORE *look under* architecture

touchtone phones
DISCUSSIONS
telephones *volume* **2** *page* **100**

Tower of London (building in London, England, U.K.)
DISCUSSIONS
London *volume* **6** *page* **16**
LEARN MORE *look under* towers

Tower of the Juche Idea (Pyongyang, North Korea)
DISCUSSIONS
Pyongyang *volume* **7** *page* **20,** photograph *volume* **7** *page* **21**
LEARN MORE *look under* towers

towers: *look under* architecture; CN Tower; Eiffel Tower; Leaning Tower of Pisa; Tower of London; Tower of the Juche Idea

trans-Alaska pipeline
DISCUSSIONS
Did you know? *volume* **2** *page* **84**

Transcaucasia (region in Europe and Asia): *look under*
places: Iran; Yerevan

transmitters
DISCUSSIONS
telephones *volume* **2** *page* **100**

transportation
ARTICLE *volume* **2** *page* **106**
LEARN MORE *look under* airplanes; automobiles; ships; spacecraft; submarines

tree frogs (animals)
DISCUSSIONS
amphibians *volume* **11** *page* **91**
frogs photograph *volume* **11** *page* **92**

trees
DISCUSSIONS
Did you know? *volume* **1** *page* **71**
leaves *volume* **1** *page* **67**
paper *volume* **2** *page* **87**
swamps *volume* **1** *page* **28**
LEARN MORE *look under*
food trees: apples; cacao; figs; jackfruit; lemons; mangoes; maple; nuts; olive; oranges; palms
other trees: bald cypress; bodhi trees; cedars; eucalyptus trees; pines; rubber trees
other things: forests; rainforests; swamps

triceratops (dinosaurs)
DISCUSSIONS
dinosaurs *volume* **1** *page* **88**

Trinity (God)
DISCUSSIONS
Christianity *volume* **5** *page* **57**

Tripoli (city in Libya)
ARTICLE *volume* **8** *page* **61**
DISCUSSIONS
atlas *volume* **13** *page* **12**
LEARN MORE *look under* Libya; North Africa

'Tristan und Isolde' (opera by Wagner)
DISCUSSIONS
opera *volume* **3** *page* **76**

Triton (moon of Neptune)
DISCUSSIONS
Neptune *volume* **2** *page* **42**

Trojan Horse, The (Greek legend): *look under*
other Greek stories: Aesop's fables; Atlas; 'Odysseus and the Cyclops'
other legends: Bunyan, Paul; dragons; 'Golem of Prague, The'; Knights of the Round Table

trumpets (musical instruments)
DISCUSSIONS
Louis Armstrong *volume* **3** *page* **39**
LEARN MORE *look under* musical instruments

Trung Sisters, Temple of the (temple in Hanoi, Vietnam)
DISCUSSIONS
Hanoi *volume* **7** *page* **42**

tsunamis, *also called* tidal waves
ARTICLE *volume* **1** *page* **50**
DISCUSSIONS
floods *volume* **1** *page* **32**
waves *volume* **1** *page* **49**
LEARN MORE *look under* weather

Tswana, *also called* Batswana (people)
DISCUSSIONS
Botswana *volume* **8** *page* **71**
LEARN MORE *look under* Botswana; peoples

tube worms
DISCUSSIONS
deep-sea life photograph *volume* **11** *page* **55**

tubers (parts of plants)
DISCUSSIONS
yams *volume* **10** *page* **33**

tulips (plants)
ARTICLE *volume* **10** *page* **9**
DISCUSSIONS
Did you know? *volume* **6** *page* **38**
LEARN MORE *look under* flowers

Turkey (country)
DISCUSSIONS
atlas *volume* **13** *page* **8**
flag *volume* **7** *page* **69**
tulips *volume* **10** *page* **9**
LEARN MORE *look under* Fertile Crescent; Istanbul

turrets (tower-like structures)
DISCUSSIONS
Did you know? *volume* **11** *page* **87**

turtles (animals)
ARTICLE *volume* **11** *page* **88**
LEARN MORE *look under* reptiles

tusks
DISCUSSIONS
elephants *volume* **12** *page* **91**
mammoths and mastodons *volume* **1** *page* **87**, illustration *volume* **1** *page* **86**
walruses *volume* **12** *page* **75**, photograph *volume* **12** *page* **74**

TV (broadcasting): *look under* television

Twain, Mark, *also called* Samuel Langhorne Clemens (American writer)
ARTICLE *volume* **4** *page* **29**
DISCUSSIONS
Did you know? *volume* **2** *page* **24**
LEARN MORE *look under* literature

'Twenty Thousand Leagues Under the Sea' (book by Verne)
DISCUSSIONS
Jules Verne *volume* **3** *page* **68**, illustration *volume* **3** *page* **69**

twins
DISCUSSIONS
Did you know? *volume* **8** *page* **20**

'Two Boys with Two Mastiffs' (painting by Goya)
DISCUSSIONS
Francisco de Goya illustration *volume* **4** *page* **15**

type, *also called* movable type (printing)
DISCUSSIONS
printing *volume* **2** *page* **90**

typhoons (wind storms): *look under* cyclones

tyrannosaurs, *also called* Tyrannosaurus rex (dinosaurs)
ARTICLE *volume* **1** *page* **92**
DISCUSSIONS
dinosaurs *volume* **1** *page* **88**
LEARN MORE *look under* fossils

UFOs, *also called* unidentified flying objects

DISCUSSIONS
extraterrestrial life *volume* **2** *page* **15**

Uganda (country)
ARTICLE *volume* **8** *page* **41**
DISCUSSIONS
atlas *volume* **13** *page* **12**
flag *volume* **8** *page* **41**
LEARN MORE *look under*
places: Eastern Africa; Kampala
animals: alligators and crocodiles; antelope; chimpanzees; elephants; giraffes; hippopotamuses; lions

ukiyo-e (Japanese art)
DISCUSSIONS
Hiroshige *volume* **3** *page* **17**

Ukraine (country)
ARTICLE *volume* **6** *page* **80**
DISCUSSIONS
atlas *volume* **13** *page* **6**
flag *volume* **6** *page* **80**
folk arts and crafts photograph *volume* **3** *page* **6**
LEARN MORE *look under* Eastern Europe; Russia

ungulates (animals with hooves): *look under* alpacas; bison; buffalo; camels; cattle; donkeys; elephants; gazelles; hippopotamuses; hooves; horses; llamas; mammoths and mastodons; pigs; sheep; tapirs; wild goats; yaks

unidentified flying objects: *look under* UFOs

uniform resource locator, *also called* URL (computer science)
DISCUSSIONS
Internet *volume* **2** *page* **80**

Union of Soviet Socialist Republics, *also called* Soviet Union, *or* U.S.S.R. (historic nation in Eurasia)
DISCUSSIONS
Cuba *volume* **9** *page* **59**
Russia *volume* **6** *page* **69**
Ukraine *volume* **6** *page* **80**
LEARN MORE *look under* communism

United Kingdom (island country)
DISCUSSIONS
atlas *volume* **13** *page* **6**
Ireland *volume* **6** *page* **24**
Mahatma Gandhi *volume* **4** *page* **95**
Nairobi *volume* **8** *page* **33**
Ottawa *volume* **9** *page* **14**
Quebec *volume* **9** *page* **17**
television *volume* **2** *page* **104**
United States of America *volume* **9** *page* **27**
Yangon *volume* **7** *page* **30**

LEARN MORE *look under*
people: Beatles, the; Carroll, Lewis; Cayley, Sir George; Christie, Agatha; Darwin, Charles; Dench, Judi; Dickens, Charles; Goodall, Jane; Halley, Edmond; Herschel, Sir William; Newton, Sir Isaac; Shakespeare, William
places: Belfast; Edinburgh; England; English Channel; London; Scotland; Stonehenge; Wales; Western Europe; White Cliffs of Dover
stories: Knights of the Round Table

United Nations (international organization)
DISCUSSIONS
U Thant *volume* **4** *page* **60**

United States of America (country)
ARTICLE *volume* **9** *page* **25**
DISCUSSIONS
atlas *volume* **13** *page* **14**
astronauts *volume* **2** *page* **19**
Cuba *volume* **9** *page* **59**
cultural melting pot *volume* **9** *page* **28**
Did you know? *volume* **1** *page* **58**
Fidel Castro *volume* **4** *page* **39**
flag *volume* **9** *page* **25**
folk music *volume* **3** *page* **31**
Grand Canyon photograph *volume* **9** *page* **33**
history *volume* **9** *page* **27**
jazz *volume* **3** *page* **35**
Liberia *volume* **8** *page* **17**
Monrovia *volume* **8** *page* **19**
nuclear power plant photograph *volume* **2** *page* **63**
Panama Canal *volume* **9** *page* **52**
peninsulas *volume* **1** *page* **22**
pigs photograph *volume* **12** *page* **65**
Puerto Rico *volume* **9** *page* **57**
Ruby Marshes in Nevada photograph *volume* **1** *page* **27**
swamps *volume* **1** *page* **28**
television *volume* **2** *page* **104**
LEARN MORE *look under*
people: Ailey, Alvin; Aldrin, Edwin E.; American Indians; Armstrong, Louis; Basie, Count; Blackwell, Elizabeth; Brooks, Gwendolyn; Burbank, Luther; Dickinson, Emily; Einstein, Albert; Ford, Henry; Henson, Jim; Keller, Helen; King, Martin Luther, Jr; Pei, I. M.; Santana, Carlos; Tallchief, Maria; Twain, Mark; Wright brothers
places: Alaska; Boston; Death Valley; Florida; Grand Canyon; Great Lakes; Hawaii; Honolulu;

New York City; Niagara Falls; Puerto Rico; Washington, D.C.
animals: armadillos; bison; coyotes; manatees; ocelots; opossums; porcupines; raccoons; wolves
stories: Bunyan, Paul

universe
ARTICLE *volume* **2** *page* **8**
DISCUSSIONS
Albert Einstein *volume* **4** *page* **74**
Kepler's model illustration *volume* **4** *page* **81**
LEARN MORE *look under* astronomy

Uranus, *also called* Georgium Sidus (planet)
ARTICLE *volume* **2** *page* **40**
DISCUSSIONS
solar system illustration *volume* **2** *page* **20**

URL (computer science): *look under* uniform resource locator

U.S.S.R. (historic nation): *look under* Union of Soviet Socialist Republics

valley glaciers (ice formations)
DISCUSSIONS
glaciers *volume* **1** *page* **54**

van Gogh, Vincent (Dutch painter)
ARTICLE *volume* **3** *page* **27**
DISCUSSIONS
Did you know? *volume* **3** *page* **9**
Netherlands, the *volume* **6** *page* **38**
LEARN MORE *look under* painting

vanilla
DISCUSSIONS
Did you know? *volume* **10** *page* **17**
LEARN MORE *look under* food; plants

vapour
DISCUSSIONS
dew *volume* **1** *page* **65**

Vatican City (city and state)
ARTICLE *volume* **6** *page* **93**
DISCUSSIONS
atlas *volume* **13** *page* **6**
Italy *volume* **6** *page* **89**
Rome *volume* **6** *page* **91**
LEARN MORE *look under* Europe

vaudeville
DISCUSSIONS
Count Basie *volume* **4** *page* **9**

Velázquez, Diego (Spanish painter)
DISCUSSIONS
paintings in the Prado Museum photograph *volume* **6** *page* **12**

Venezuela (country)
DISCUSSIONS
atlas *volume* **13** *page* **17**
Did you know? *volume* **4** *page* **88**
rainforests photograph *volume* **1** *page* **24**
LEARN MORE *look under* South America
people: Bolívar, Simón

Venus (planet)
ARTICLE *volume* **2** *page* **33**
DISCUSSIONS
solar system illustration *volume* **2** *page* **20**
LEARN MORE *look under* planets

Venus fly trap (plant)
DISCUSSIONS
carnivorous plants *volume* **10** *page* **19,** illustration *volume* **10** *page* **19**

Verne, Jules (French writer)
ARTICLE *volume* **3** *page* **68**
LEARN MORE *look under* literature; spacecraft; submarines

Vesuvius, Mount (volcano in Italy)
DISCUSSIONS
volcanoes *volume* **1** *page* **15**
LEARN MORE *look under* Italy; mountains

viceroy butterflies (insects)
DISCUSSIONS
Did you know? *volume* **11** *page* **63**

'Victoria' (ship)
DISCUSSIONS
Ferdinand Magellan illustration *volume* **4** *page* **101**

Victoria, Lake (lake in Africa)
DISCUSSIONS
Africa *volume* **8** *page* **7**
Uganda *volume* **8** *page* **41**
LEARN MORE *look under* Africa; lakes

Victoria amazonica (plants)
DISCUSSIONS
Colombia *volume* **9** *page* **71**
LEARN MORE *look under* plants; water lilies

Victoria Falls (waterfall in Africa)
ARTICLE *volume* **8** *page* **92**

DISCUSSIONS
atlas *volume* **13** *page* **12**
Zimbabwe *volume* **8** *page* **89**
LEARN MORE *look under* Southern Africa; waterfalls

Victoria Falls Bridge (bridge between Zambia and Zimbabwe)
DISCUSSIONS
Victoria Falls *volume* **8** *page* **92**
LEARN MORE *look under*
other bridges: Charles Bridge; Halfpenny Bridge

Vienna (city in Austria)
ARTICLE *volume* **6** *page* **51**
DISCUSSIONS
atlas *volume* **13** *page* **6**
LEARN MORE *look under*
people: Mozart, Wolfgang Amadeus
places: Austria

Vienna Boys' Choir
DISCUSSIONS
Vienna *volume* **6** *page* **51**

Vienna State Opera (Austria)
DISCUSSIONS
Vienna *volume* **6** *page* **51,** photograph *volume* **6** *page* **51**

Vietnam (country)
ARTICLE *volume* **7** *page* **40**
DISCUSSIONS
atlas *volume* **13** *page* **8**
LEARN MORE *look under*
places: Hanoi; Southeast Asia
religion: Daoism

Vietnam War
DISCUSSIONS
Hanoi *volume* **7** *page* **42**
Vietnam *volume* **7** *page* **40**

Viking (U.S. space probes)
DISCUSSIONS
Mars *volume* **2** *page* **35,** photograph *volume* **2** *page* **35**
LEARN MORE *look under* exploration; spacecraft

Vikings, *also called* Norsemen (Norse people)
ARTICLE *volume* **4** *page* **62**
DISCUSSIONS
Did you know? *volume* **9** *page* **9**
LEARN MORE *look under* exploration; Norse mythology; Scandinavia

vines (plants)
DISCUSSIONS
grapes *volume* **10** *page* **25**
LEARN MORE *look under* plants

water: *look under* acid rain; Antarctica; clouds; dew; floods; glaciers; icebergs; marshes; oasis; oceans; rivers; swamps; water power; waterfalls

water buffalo, *also called* Indian buffalo (animals)
DISCUSSIONS
buffalo *volume* **12** *page* **49,**
photograph *volume* **12** *page* **48**

water lilies (plants)
ARTICLE *volume* **10** *page* **15**
LEARN MORE *look under* flowers; Victoria amazonica

water power
ARTICLE *volume* **2** *page* **67**
LEARN MORE *look under* nuclear energy; technology; thermal power; water; wind power

water wheels: *look under* waterwheels

waterfalls
DISCUSSIONS
rivers *volume* **1** *page* **31**
water power *volume* **2** *page* **67**
LEARN MORE *look under*
waterfalls: Angel Falls; Niagara Falls; Victoria Falls

waterways: *look under* Bosporus; Dardanelles; English Channel; Gibraltar, Strait of; Magellan, Strait of; Panama Canal; rivers; Suez Canal

waterwheels
DISCUSSIONS
water power *volume* **2** *page* **67,**
photograph *volume* **2** *page* **67**

waves
ARTICLE *volume* **1** *page* **49**
DISCUSSIONS
sand *volume* **1** *page* **18**
LEARN MORE *look under* echoes; tsunamis

weather: *look under* clouds; cyclones; dew; rainbows; thunder and lightning; tsunamis; waves; wind power

weaving (cloth production)
ARTICLE *volume* **2** *page* **108**
DISCUSSIONS
Did you know? *volume* **2** *page* **79**
LEARN MORE *look under* technology

Web (computer science): *look under* Internet and the World Wide Web

weft (weaving)
DISCUSSIONS
weaving *volume* **2** *page* **108,**
photograph *volume* **2** *page* **109**

Welles, Orson (American actor, director, and writer)
DISCUSSIONS
Did you know? *volume* **2** *page* **93**

Wellington (city in New Zealand)
ARTICLE *volume* **7** *page* **101**
DISCUSSIONS
atlas *volume* **13** *page* **10**
LEARN MORE *look under* New Zealand

Wenceslas Square (square in Prague, Czech Republic)
DISCUSSIONS
Prague *volume* **6** *page* **55**

West Africa
DISCUSSIONS
Vodun photograph *volume* **5** *page* **93**
LEARN MORE *look under*
places: Accra; Dakar; Ghana; Guinea; Liberia; Monrovia; Nigeria; Senegal
animals: manatees
stories: 'Ananse and the Wisdom Pot'; 'Monkey Court, The'

West Indies (island group in the Atlantic Ocean)
ARTICLE *volume* **9** *page* **54**
DISCUSSIONS
atlas *volume* **13** *page* **14**
LEARN MORE *look under*
places: Cuba; Haiti; Puerto Rico; Tobago
things: bananas; manatees; Vodun

West Pakistan (country): *look under* Pakistan

Western Australia (state in Australia)
ARTICLE *volume* **7** *page* **97**
DISCUSSIONS
atlas *volume* **13** *page* **10**
LEARN MORE *look under* Australia

Western Europe: *look under*
countries: Belgium; England; France; Ireland; Netherlands, the; Portugal; Scotland; Spain; United Kingdom
other places: English Channel; Stonehenge

Western Wall, *also called* Wailing Wall (prayer site in Jerusalem)
DISCUSSIONS
Jerusalem *volume* **7** *page* **77,**
photograph *volume* **7** *page* **76**
LEARN MORE *look under* architecture

Westminster Abbey (church in London, England, U.K.)
DISCUSSIONS
London *volume* **6** *page* **16**

wetlands: *look under* marshes; swamps

whale shark (fish)
DISCUSSIONS
fish *volume* **11** *page* **35**
sharks *volume* **11** *page* **43,**
photograph *volume* **11** *page* **43**
LEARN MORE *look under* sharks

whales
ARTICLE *volume* **12** *page* **76**
DISCUSSIONS
Antarctica *volume* **1** *page* **11**
Did you know? *volume* **1** *page* **40,**
volume **12** *page* **7**
LEARN MORE *look under* dolphins; mammals; manatees; marine animals; walruses

wheat (grain)
ARTICLE *volume* **10** *page* **75**
LEARN MORE *look under* grasses

White Cliffs of Dover (cliffs in England, U.K.)
DISCUSSIONS
chalk *volume* **1** *page* **83,** photograph *volume* **1** *page* **82**
LEARN MORE *look under* England; English Channel

white-handed gibbons, *also called* Malayan lars (apes)
DISCUSSIONS
gibbons photograph *volume* **12** *page* **13**

'Why Possum's Tail Is Bare' (Cherokee folktale)
ARTICLE *volume* **5** *page* **36**
LEARN MORE *look under*
other American stories: Bunyan, Paul; 'How Crow Brought Daylight to the World'; 'Rabbit Throws Away His Sandal'
other folktales: 'Ananse and the Wisdom Pot'; 'How Kangaroo Got His Tail'; 'Monkey Court, The'; 'Poor Man and the Flask of Oil, The'; 'Tiger in the Trap, The'; 'Yeh-Shen'

wieners (sausages)
DISCUSSIONS
Did you know? *volume* **6** *page* **48**
LEARN MORE *look under* food

wild goats
ARTICLE *volume* **12** *page* **58**
DISCUSSIONS
sheep *volume* **12** *page* **57**
LEARN MORE *look under* ungulates